WILLS
  A Dead Giveaway

Wills

A DEAD GIVEAWAY

by Millie Considine and Ruth Pool

Doubleday & Company, Inc., Garden City, New York

Library of Congress Cataloging in Publication Data
Considine, Millie.
   Wills; a dead giveaway.
   1. Wills—United States—Anecdotes, facetiae, satire, etc. I. Pool, Ruth, joint
author. II. Title.
KF758.C65   346′.73′0540207
ISBN 0-385-08277-0
Library of Congress Catalog Card Number 73-18775

Charles Atlas—Excerpted from *Trusts & Estates*, April 1973. Copyright 1973, Communication Channels, Inc., 461 Eighth Avenue, New York, N.Y. 10001
Helen deYoung Cameron—Excerpted from *Trusts & Estates*, January 1970. Copyright 1970, Communication Channels, Inc., 461 Eighth Avenue, New York, N.Y. 10001
Joseph Valachi—Excerpted from *Trusts & Estates*, November 1971. Copyright 1971, Communication Channels, Inc., 461 Eighth Avenue, New York, N.Y. 10001
The Greer Case by David W. Peck, published by Cornerstone Library-Courtroom Series. *The Recluse of Herald Square* by Joseph A. Cox, published by Macmillan Company, New York, 1964, Encyclopaedia Britannica (1968, vols. 16, 19, and 20). *The Show Business Nobody Knows* by Earl Wilson, published by Cowles Publications. *It's All News to Me* by Bob Considine, published by Meredith Press. *The Last Will and Testament* published by Robert A. Farmer and Associates.

Special thanks for assistance given us to: Peter McLaughlin, register of wills, Washington, D.C.; Winifred Scott, register of wills for Montgomery County, Maryland; Julius F. Chase of the wills department of Phillips, Nizer, Benjamin, Krim and Ballon; Surrogate Judge Samuel DiFalco; Fred Ingram of Morgan Guaranty Trust Company of New York; William A. Koshland, president of Alfred A. Knopf, Inc.; Chief Judge of the U. S. District Court Matthew F. McGuire (for his story on Joseph Holt); feature writer Edward Boykin (for his story on Stephen Decatur); Stuart Rasmussen, librarian of the San Francisco *Examiner;* Charles Gould, publisher of the San Francisco *Examiner;* Louise Metzger, librarian of King Features; Helen Griffiths of the New York *Times;* Dave Woods of the Baltimore *Sun;* Thomas White of the Baltimore *News American;* Sam Bornstein of the Boston *Herald American;* Donald Goodenow of the Los Angeles *Herald Examiner;* William Bellamy of the San Antonio *Light;* the New Bedford *Standard Times;* the New York *Daily News* "morgue" and its librarian Joseph McCarthy; John Winkler, official biographer of F. W. Woolworth in his book *Five and Ten;* Robert Peel, editorial counselor of the First Church of Christ, Scientist; Sandra Ogle, Assistant Director of Public Relations for the Cabrini Health Care Center; Florence Hill, Clark Roberts, and Melvin Robbins; Thomas H. Hamilton, special advisor to the Kamehameha Schools/Bernice Pauahi Bishop Estate; and finally to Judge Harry T. Shafer of Compton, California, who gave us the title.

Contents

WILLS
A Dead Giveaway

Chapter 1

Where There's a Will

The first will known to exist is that of Nek'ure, carved on the wall of a tomb around the year 26 A.D. "While standing on my own two feet and not ailing in any respect," he disposed of fourteen towns and two estates to be divided among his wife, three children, and one woman.

In the days of savages the possessions of a deceased person went to whoever got there first and grabbed them; thus the family stuck around pretty close so as to be the first to grab the deceased's effects.

Later came the days of powerful monasteries and Church courts, and often clergymen called in to perform the last rites were asked to write down the wishes of the dying man, being scribes.

Along came the old feudal lords, who changed the ideas of property by force of arms and developed the plan of having all property of a deceased person vest in his feudal lord. This rule was enforced until 1541, when, under Henry VIII, the statute was enacted that gave the absolute right to dispose of real estate by will. Thereupon a distinct custom and rules of law were built up by means of which a person could dispose of property at his death according to his own wishes.

The disposition of his property by a deceased person has been a fascinating topic of conversation ever since. "What did he leave?" and "Who got it?" are almost the first questions asked when one hears of the death of a friend or celebrity.

This book is about some of the interesting, amusing, fey, charming, vengeful, or downright nutty wills we've come across, about the people who wrote those wills, and who benefited, and about the litigations and side effects sometimes involved in simple, well-meaning wills.

There is no telling what goes through a person's mind when he comes to write his last will and testament. The norm is to express love and gratitude for those left behind by leaving them legacies. But sometimes due to senility, vindictiveness, momentary anger, helplessness, or even a sense of humor, the bequests take unforeseen and unlikely turns.

The contents of a will depend entirely on the health, mental condition, and surroundings of the testator. Very often a perfectly legal, straightforward, and intelligent will made out in a lawyer's office in the testator's prime of life is scrapped during the last days of illness or senility and a totally different one is substituted that is unfair and even ridiculous; unfair in the sense that long-suffering, hard-working secretaries, maids, cooks, chauffeurs, and companions who have spent years taking care of their employer, and been promised that they in turn would be taken care of for life in the will, are dropped in favor of a new acquaintance, nurse, doctor, lawyer, or distant relative.

Such was the case in the will of the aged remaining member of a team of dancing sisters famous in the first part of this century. In her last will, executed in the extremity of her final illness, she cut off her servants and companion, some of whom had been with her for forty years and given her care far beyond the call of duty during her many illnesses, with five thousand dollars each. The bulk of her estate went to a long-estranged adopted niece and a croupier in Las Vegas, who had gone out of his way to be nice to her during her last gambling spree before her death.

Very often hate dictates a will, rather than love. A wealthy furrier who died recently in New York left a will worded in such a way it could only make his children turn on each other —therefore he must have hated *them*. Another late construction tycoon, who had spent years trying to impress everyone with his great love for his beautiful actress wife, rewrote his will on his deathbed leaving everything possible to two nephews he had seen very little of rather than to his "beloved" wife. His way of showing she wasn't so beloved after all, perhaps? Or did the nephews move in at the last minute, as so often happens, and convince him he should take care of his own blood relatives? It took the bewildered widow years to straighten it all out and even get her dower rights.

A will that warms the cockles of the heart was that of a Brooklyn woman who remembered, financially, every person who had shown her kindness, from waitresses to milkmen to neighbors. But she showed a very human trait, too, in making out the will. She had two nephews, and she willed fifty thousand dollars to the one who had sent her a Christmas card, and left only twenty-five thousand dollars to the one who did not send a card. One shudders to think how many times the nephew who inherited the lesser amount must have figuratively kicked himself for not investing a quarter in a card for dear old Auntie at Christmastime.

Once in a while a will reveals a lifetime of frustration. Apparently the frustration of Martin Calhoun Burghard was that a book of verses he wrote never got published. His will, dated December 8, 1930, goes like this: 1. All of my books, notebooks and personal effects to Oscar B. Strackbein. 2. My body to some body of students for dissection and for study. I leave the disposition of same to Oscar Strackbein. If he can dispose of the body to advantage, he is requested to do so and use the moneys in publishing my single book of verse. In case no financial gain is possible, he is to contribute it to such body of students as he so desires. 3. My skin is to be used to make a binding for my book of verse. Under no circumstances is my body to be disposed of unless the recipients return the skin in such shape that it can be used for a book binding. 4. My insurance policies belong to my Mother. 5. If the sale of my book of verse is considerable, the first $300 profit is to go to Miss Fannie York for services rendered me on this night. (This No. 5 was scratched out in the will "due to failure of young lady to meet me. Am quite disappointed.")

Quite often a lawyer manages to insinuate himself or his

family, or both, into a last-minute will, or gets himself appointed executor, which provision gives him emoluments as well as complete control over the estate. This happened in the case of one of our best-known actresses, who at the last minute cut her own sister out of her will and left a considerable amount to the lawyer's children. Another legendary performer left to her lawyer's wife jewelry that she had long since promised to someone else.

An internationally famous male singer disregarded his late wife's explicit instructions regarding the disposition of her jewelry to various close women friends (he was the executor of the will) and kept the jewelry. He remarried a very young woman shortly after his wife's death and generously gave the new wife all of his late wife's jewelry. She left him—taking along all the jewelry—a short time later.

All of his relatives, who hated and distrusted each other, had their own batteries of lawyers lined up to fight the will of an eccentric Texas multimillionaire long before he died. Sure enough, he cut off his namesake son with one dollar and wasn't much kinder to the other relatives. But all those lawyers couldn't do much about the fact that he left most of his four hundred million dollar estate as a charity foundation.

It was generally agreed, certainly among some of the top employees in the old man's multiple business interests, that he had a pretty good reason for cutting off his son. The old man was in the hospital suffering from a bad gall bladder, and because of his age and serious illness, it was assumed he was about to die. At least his son assumed that, whereupon the son immediately fired the top executives in all the various businesses, to be replaced by employees of his own choice. But lo and behold, his father rose from his sickbed and went home. When some of the employees involved came to turn in their resignations personally, and the old man learned what his son had done, he immediately changed his will, cut the son off with one dollar, and severed relations with him.

The amount of money to be bequeathed does not dictate the length of a will. A British lady who died in the 1920s left a will over 1,000 pages long, yet the amount involved was only $100,000. Margaret Lacey, in January of 1902, wrote her will on a roll of wallpaper 15 feet long, with most of the bequests $100 or less. Joseph Keefe, who died in 1931 but wrote his will in 1905, had a much shorter will. He simply wrote "Legal Airs" on a will form. So he didn't spell so well, the will was still probated and the legal heirs benefited. Mrs. Agnes Burley, a waitress most of her life, wrote her last will and testament on two paper napkins. At stake was her $34,198 estate.

Many a dog, cat, or bird has been the beneficiary of a will, which is a sad commentary on the kind of life the deceased must have had among *people*. One Washington, D.C., lady left her estate for the upkeep of her pet parrakeet by her black housekeeper, who was allowed to maintain the home as long as the parrakeet lived. After that the money was to go to a school. One day the old black woman showed up at the register of wills office in Washington, D.C., carrying a box containing the dead parrakeet. The clerk who talked to her was so impressed with her honesty he felt like suggesting she hide the dead bird and buy another parrakeet so she could continue to be supported.

The aid of fortune tellers, spiritualists, palmists, etc., has been enlisted by many a potential legatee to track down a lost will—one in which he was sure he was mentioned favorably. This ploy actually worked in the case of one widow, whom we'll call Mrs. Jones, who had seen her husband's will leaving her everything and knew it existed. But that will was nowhere to be found after her husband's death. The only one found was a much earlier one, written before their marriage, leaving everything to the deceased's sister. Mrs. Jones was convinced the sister had found the later will and hidden or destroyed it. Despite that thought, Mrs. Jones gave the sister a painting of a desert and mountain scene belonging to her husband—a painting the sister had always admired and coveted.

About a year after her husband died, Mrs. Jones was at ·a party where a fortune teller was brought in to tell the guests'

fortunes, just for a gag. That particular fortune teller's gim-
mick was to have the person whose fortune she was telling
throw a bunch of stones on a table; then the fortune was told
from the way the stones fell. Crazy? But wait. When Mrs. Jones
tossed her stones, the fortune teller said, "You are worried
about the whereabouts of an important document. I see an
apartment in Greenwich Village where one walks up three
steps from the living room to a hallway (an exact description
of the sister's apartment). Hanging on the wall there is a picture or painting of desert and mountains. The document is
hidden behind that picture." It was.

Chapter 2

A Shubert Production

The saga of the Shubert family, theatrical producers and theater owners, would make as good a play as any of the productions that have appeared on their stages. The cast includes John Shubert, his father J. J. Shubert, his uncles Lee and Sam Shubert, his mother Catherine Shubert, his first wife Kerttu Shubert, and the mother of his two children, Nancy Mae Eyerman, with minor roles played by various lawyers and other relatives.

A dramatic first scene would be the funeral of John Shubert, held Nov. 21, 1962, at the Majestic Theatre in New York and attended by twelve hundred people. The setting of the current show playing there then, *Camelot,* was covered with black velour drops. A mahogany coffin covered with a blanket of American Beauty roses occupied the center of the lighted stage. Beside the coffin were a leather chair and a lectern. The widow, Kerttu Helene Ecklund Shubert, a former singer and dancer in Broadway musicals, occupied the chair. Roger Stevens, producer and chairman of the National Cultural Center in Washington, stood at the lectern and was the sole speaker. Stevens said Shubert had left instructions for his services to be conducted this way, and read off a list of the important dates in Shubert's life, which Shubert had written personally. After that Stevens gave his eulogy.

In our play, as Stevens is speaking, the set turns around to the next set, and we go into the life of the man in the coffin. As the play progresses we see that John Shubert married Kerttu in 1937, served in World War II, and was handed the reins of the family's huge business in the late 1950s, after having produced several shows himself.

In the background was the continuing harassment of the demand of the four executors of Lee Shubert, who died in 1953, for an accounting from John and his father J.J., and a federal antitrust action requiring the Shuberts to divest themselves of twelve of their theaters in six cities, which they agreed to in 1956. The four executors of Lee's estate suing for half the assets were two nephews, Milton Shubert and Lawrence Shubert Lawrence; a niece, Sylvia Golde; and a former lawyer for the Shubert brothers, William Klein.

While administering the theatrical enterprises with their problems, John Shubert was having a few problems of his own. He divorced his wife Kerttu on January 9, 1961, in Chihuahua, Mexico, and a few days later he purportedly married Nancy Mae Eyerman, by whom he already had a daughter. A son was born to them later. It was while John was on a train enroute to Clearwater, Florida, to have Thanksgiving dinner with Nancy and the children, that he died of a heart attack, at the age of fifty-three.

Kerttu contended that her marriage to John had not been terminated and that as late as April 1962, she and Shubert filed their income tax jointly, and lived together at 17 West 54th Street. Nancy contended that at the time of his death she and John were preparing to move into a New York apartment. Both women claimed to be John's legal widow.

In a will dated December 8, 1960, John left the bulk of his estate, estimated at six hundred thousand dollars, to his widow, Mrs. Kerttu Helene Shubert, of 17 West 54th Street. John's mother Catherine supported Nancy's claim, stating that her son during his lifetime had acknowledged to her that he had divorced Kerttu, had married Nancy Eyerman, and that Sarah and John were his children. She said she recognized the children as his, and they recognized her as their grandmother. She asserted that John had executed another will during the summer of 1962, just before leaving for Europe. An unwitnessed carbon copy of the purported second will was found in a safe deposit box and was dated June 26, 1962. The copy named Mrs. Catherine Shubert sole executor and the guardian of his

two small children, and ceded most of his estate to Nancy
Mae Eyerman. It set up trust funds for the two children from
funds expected to be realized from John's book *Shubert Alley*,
and left bequests to Lawrence Shubert Lawrence, a second
cousin, and three godchildren. The original of this carbon copy
will was not found, so it held no water. The carbon was unwitnessed, and an array of lawyers declared the signature was
a forgery.

Mrs. Catherine Shubert finally withdrew her objections to
the December 8, 1960, will, and it was filed for probate.
A compromise settlement was reached between the two
women claiming to be Shubert's widow, and Kerttu was
awarded the bulk of the estate. Nancy Mae Eyerman's two
children were recognized as Shubert's legitimate children, and
each received $12,500. Also at stake in the litigation was the
$15 million estate that was expected to accrue to John after
the death of his father J.J. The children surrendered any claim
to that expected estate. The Mexican divorce obtained by
John from Kerttu and his subsequent marriage in Mexico to
Nancy were voided. A Fifth Avenue apartment and a home in
Connecticut were ceded to John's mother Catherine. Nancy
agreed in the settlement to refrain from any future use of the
name Shubert and never to claim to have been married to
John. She received two insurance policies for $25,000, each
of which had been made out to her by John.

The scene where the two "widows" faced each other at the
settlement hearing would be a dramatic one. Nancy Mae, a
tall, slim, dark-haired woman, wept soundlessly and kept
dabbing her eyes, but regained her composure when she
walked to the witness stand and declared that she approved
of the settlement. Kerttu, a slight, blond woman, sat in a wheel-
chair with her broken leg in a plaster cast. Both wore wedding
rings. Neither woman would comment afterward, but Nancy's
lawyer said Nancy had achieved her main objective, to have
her children recognized as legitimate.

Now to the ending of the subplot. John's father J.J. died
just a year after John died, without ever knowing that his son

was dead. The legal action of Lee Shubert's executors demanding an accounting, begun in 1954, was finally settled in 1966. A state Supreme Court justice ruled that the estate of Lee Shubert was entitled to receive about $28 million from the estate of his brother J.J. Justice John Flynn said the partnership between the two brothers was worth $33.5 million when Lee died in 1953, and that the Lee Shubert estate was entitled to half the value of the partnership, or $16.7 million, plus 6 percent interest for every year between when Lee died in 1953 and J.J. died in 1963, more than $11 million. Both Lee's and J.J.'s wills benefited the Sam Shubert Foundation, established by Lee and J.J. in honor of their brother Sam, who started the Shubert enterprises and was killed in a train wreck in 1905. The foundation makes grants to theatrical organizations, persons interested in theater careers, and to philanthropic and educational groups.

The appeals, litigations, and tax assessments that followed would be of no interest in our play, which would probably end with the scene of the two widows facing each other in the courtroom. Or perhaps a more dramatic ending would be to return to the first scene: the funeral. The coffin of John is in the center of the stage, Kerttu occupies a chair next to the coffin, and perhaps Nancy Mae is sitting in a shadowed box on the side of the theater, weeping silently, as Roger Stevens continues on with his anecdotes about the life of John.

Chapter 3

A Case of Identity

When an ancient ninety-three-year-old woman with matted gray hair opened the door of her room in the Herald Square Hotel, where she had been a recluse for twenty-four years, and called a chambermaid to say her sister was sick, she opened the door on the world at last, and on the strange story of Ida Wood, a story that made headlines and ended in over a thousand people claiming her fortune; for a fortune she had, hidden among the incredible rubble of the two rooms she, her sister Mary, and her "daughter" Emma had inhabited all those years without ever stepping out or allowing anyone to enter. The door had only been opened, previously, to allow elevator boys to hand in delicatessen food the women had ordered, and once, three years before, to allow Emma to be taken out to a hospital where she died.

The chambermaid called a doctor, who regarded the dismally littered place incredulously as he walked into the bedroom to see the patient. The patient was patently dying of cancer, but when the doctor suggested she be moved to a hospital, the old woman said "No, I don't want her moved—you can go now." The doctor said he had to have her name and the name of the dying sister, to make a report. "I'm Ida Wood; my husband was Benjamin Wood, and his brother was mayor of New York. My sister's name is Mary Mayfield, and she's ninety-one years old." Something prompted the doctor to take another look at the patient, and he saw that she was dead. "Oh, dear, now she'll have to be buried, and that will cost money," complained Ida.

The manager of the hotel was called in and told to locate an undertaker. He brought in a Mr. McDonnell, whose funeral home was nearby. They could make no sense about funeral arrangements with Ida, but finally she said "Call Judge O'Brien —he always handled matters for my husband, and I don't see why he can't handle this for me." They found a Morgan J. O'Brien, Jr., listed in the directory and called the number. Mr. O'Brien answered the phone and said the judge was his father, who was in Florida, but he would call his father for instructions. After talking to his father, young O'Brien immediately called McDonnell and instructed him to go ahead with the funeral. He also called one of the firm's lawyers, Harold G. Wentworth, a specialist in handling estates, and said to meet him at the Herald Square Hotel. They met there, and that was the end of Ida's private world.

When the two men entered the room, Ida sat down in a rocking chair and lighted a long, thin cigar. During her ramblings, she hinted that she had a good deal of cash hidden in the bedroom, said her daughter and her sister had both had money that they willed to her, and she showed them some Union Pacific bonds and uncashed dividend checks. Then she told them to get out.

O'Brien's firm decided to look into the sources of the wealth Ida had hinted at. They learned that the sisters had owned about $175,000 worth of stock and hadn't cashed their dividend checks for years. They also found that when Ida had sold her late husband's newspaper, the *Daily News*, to Frank Munsey, the price was over $250,000. A bank official remembered that one day in 1907, just before the panic, Ida had closed her account, putting nearly a million dollars in her net bag and marching out. Realizing that Ida must have a huge fortune, the lawyers concluded they'd better protect her interests by engaging guards to be posted outside Ida's room on a twenty-four-hour-a-day basis, to keep out unauthorized persons and keep an eye on Ida. They also had Mary's body taken from the apartment, where it had lain for two days, and arranged for the burial. Nobody attended the funeral, not not even Ida. Mary was not embalmed and was buried in the clothes she died in.

The lawyers' relations with Ida became more and more difficult, so they started looking for relatives who could protect her interests. They found Otis Wood, a son of Fernando Wood (who had been mayor of New York) and therefore a nephew of Ida's husband Ben, presumably Ida's closest living relative. Otis Wood and other Wood relatives were rebuffed in their efforts to talk to Ida, and asked the attorneys to have a psychiatrist examine her. Two doctors came and won her confidence to the extent that she gave them a tour of the suite, told them of her life with her husband, said that she had cardboard boxes filled with jewels and $385,000 in cash, and that someone had climbed in through the transom and stolen many of her treasures. Her incoherent ramblings convinced the doctors that she was incapable of taking care of herself and her possessions. Otis Wood instituted a proceeding to have Ida declared legally incompetent, and meantime a special guardian was appointed to protect Ida's interests, a lawyer named Edward Corcoran. Corcoran gained her confidence and persuaded her to let him put some of her money in a safety deposit box, but she was cagey about where the rest of the money and jewels were hidden.

By now a legal storm began to brew; for by now two sets of Woods were in the act, both potential inheritors of Ida's fortune. One faction consisted of Otis and three other sons of Fernando, all New York businessmen, and several grandchildren. The other faction consisted of Ben's descendants by his first marriage to Catherine Davidson. There were five of them, headed by Blanche Wood Shields. This faction contended its members were direct descendants, not collateral relatives, as were nephews or grandnephews because they were the children of Ben by a previous marriage. Both factions agreed that nothing could be done unless Ida was declared incompetent and a committee was appointed to take care of her affairs. A sheriff's jury declared Ida incompetent, and Otis was named "Committee of her person and her property," meaning he was now responsible for Ida's physical and financial welfare and was accountable to the court. Otis hired day and night nurses to stay with Ida, and forcibly moved her to a duplicate suite on the floor below so her apartment could be searched.

Both Wood factions, with their lawyers in tow, conducted a search through the unbelievable rubble of the apartment. A crumbling yellow shoebox under a pile of newspapers yielded $247,000, mostly in $5,000 and $1,000 bills. Trunks yielded hundreds of old dresses, ball gowns, furs, and hats of another era. The search next turned to a warehouse, where Ida and her sister had forty trunks stored. These contained only silks, clothes, mementos, hundreds of cakes of soap from different hotels, a collection of rare and valuable books, and bundles of correspondence between Ben and Ida. But they couldn't find that second million dollars they were seeking. They even had Mary's body exhumed to see if the money was in her casket, but it wasn't.

While all this was going on, Ida was being comfortably cared for by two nurses, who were instructed to write down every word she said. She begrudged the money spent for her meals, and the nurses had to lie about the cost of them. Ida was given a $5 bill as a sop, and she clutched it to her as she sat in her rocking chair smoking her cigar, rubbing Vaseline on her face to keep it smooth, and reminiscing about her life. And quite a life it had been, too. She'd married a rich man, Benjamin Wood, who served in the New York State Senate and the U. S. House of Representatives, and she had been very active in the social and political life of New York. Since her husband owned the old *Daily News* and her brother-in-law Fernando was the mayor of New York, Ida was right in the thick of all the political intrigues of the time. Both brothers favored the South rather than Lincoln in the Civil War, and were quite rabid about it. Though a seemingly fragile beauty, Ida was an astute businesswoman and managed to get everything Ben owned in her name so that he died penniless and didn't even have a will to probate. Ben was a compulsive gambler, but Ida made him give her a percentage of his winnings and even charged waiting time in her carriage outside the gambling places. She took over the *Daily News* and tried to run it herself after her husband died, but eventually sold it to Frank Munsey.

When the reminiscences would run down, Ida would take a nap, and that's when the nurses got busy. They found a fabulous diamond and emerald necklace in a moldy box of crackers Ida kept by the bed. They also noticed a lump under her skirt while Ida was sleeping; they investigated and uncovered a bag tied around her waist containing $500,000, mostly in $10,000 bills.

By now the newspapers were vitally interested in Ida's story, and reporters and photographers practically camped in the halls of the hotel. When they wrote that Ida had given the name of Mayfield when she married Ben Wood and had been described as the daughter of Judge Henry Mayfield, a rich sugar planter from New Orleans, they gave the story a big play. That caused the Mayfields of Louisiana to get into the act too. The first Mayfield claimants were Lindsay Mayfield, manager of a grocery store in New Orleans, and his nephew Earl Mayfield, who claimed that they too were descendants of Judge Henry Mayfield. Letters from other Mayfields began to pour in, claiming relationship.

In March Ida caught a cold that turned into pneumonia, and on March 12 she died of a heart attack. On the death certificate the doctor wrote: name of father, Thomas Henry Mayfield; birthplace, Ireland; name of mother, Ann Mary Crawford; birthplace, Ireland. He got this information from Otis and the nurses. How true this information might be was the subject of the next search, the search for the identity of Ida Wood. Her battle was ended, but the battle of the heirs was just beginning. The lawyers began piecing her story together. She'd written Ben Wood a letter in 1857, when she'd arrived in New York, saying she had heard about him from a girlfriend and would like to meet him on intimate terms. They did meet and fall in love. Whether they were married secretly then, or whether she remained his mistress for ten years until their official recorded marriage in 1867 is not known. They claimed Emma, who had lived in the Herald Square with Ida until her death, as their daughter, but when Ben made out a will giving Emma, "his daughter," six thousand dollars a year, he also wrote the priest who had officiated at his marriage saying Emma was really Ida's sister but had been brought up to think she was their daughter. That will, and eighteen later wills Ben wrote, came to naught, as Ben died penniless in 1900. Ida had it all, in her name.

Apparently Ida, Mary, and Emma traveled around Europe for seven years after Ben died before going into complete seclusion in the Herald Square Hotel, in 1907. Emma had always been passed off as much younger than she was, and the pretense was easy because she was tiny because of curvature of the spine. She'd actually made a debut at the age of thirty-five, but was passed off as twenty-five, and their frequent and prolonged travels were given as the reason for the delay in having the debut.

When Ida died, the O'Brien firm offered for probate the will she made on July 9, 1889, written in her hand and witnessed by Ben Wood and R. F. McCormack. The will left her entire estate to her sister Mary E. W. Mayfield and her "daughter" Emma Wood to be divided equally, and Mary was named sole executrix. When Otis Wood filed his application for probate of the will, the other faction, led by Mrs. Shields, petitioned the court to have one of their group appointed temporary administrator of Ida's estate. Surrogate Foley granted temporary letters of administration to Ben's great-grandson Henry Wood, jointly with Bankers Trust Company. This was a victory for the Shields faction.

Proof of Ben's signature on Ida's will could be found, but no proof was available of the handwriting of the unidentified R. F. McCormack, so Foley denied probate of Ida's will, though holding that the signature of Ida was established as authentic. That last statement would have a significant part in the case. By then more than two hundred claimants had claimed varying degrees of kinship to Ida. Foley then directed the public administrator to apply for letters of administration of the estate, which letters were granted in 1934.

Now it was the job of Joseph Cox, as counsel to the public administrator, to find out who Ida Wood really was. When the public administrator's efforts to ascertain the identity or whereabouts of heirs or next of kin prove fruitless, he gives public notice of the settlement of the estate by the surrogate. The balance of the estate, after paying off obligations, then is turned over to the city treasury, and five years later to the state. During this period or any time later, persons proving a right to the estate or any part of it are entitled to payment. Cox started examining the voluminous records to obtain clues as to who Ida might be, including everything that littered Ida's rooms at the hotel, writings found in the stored trunks, and hundreds of letters from claimants.

The first clue to identity came in a letter Cox found that had been written by Father Young, who married the couple, asking for dispensation for a mixed marriage between Benjamin Wood and Ida Ellen *Walsh.* Then why had the marriage register been signed Ida Ellen Walsh Mayfield? Where did the name Walsh fit into Ida's picture? Other puzzling documents found in Ida's room also linked her to the name Walsh: an undertaker's receipt given to a Mr. Thomas Walsh for the burial of his son in 1848 in a cemetery in Cambridge, Massachusetts; another receipt given to Mother Russell of the Sisters of Mercy in San Francisco for the burial of a Thomas Walsh in Mount Calvary Cemetery there in 1864 turned up. Cox also found in Ida's effects two sheets of paper giving initials, dates, and places. Cox felt if he could decipher those hieroglyphics he could unravel the mystery of Ida's identity. One of the most valuable documents among Ida's effects was a rose-colored notebook. It contained Ida's comments on her mother's death in Glasgow, her burial there, and a Glasgow death certificate showing that her mother's maiden name was Ann Mary Crawford and that she was the widow of Henry Mayfield, sugar planter. Ida had the body exhumed and brought back to New York. The notebook also had a notation that bore an obvious relation to the receipt for the burial of Thomas Walsh in San Francisco. It said "Father arrived in Calif. Aug. 6, 1862, died Nov. 9, 1864, buried in Mount Cal-

vary Cemetery, Calif." This indicated that Thomas Walsh was
Ida's father. But at Calvary Cemetery in New York the family
history Ida had engraved on the monument stated that
Thomas Henry Mayfield was her father. Could she have had
both a father and a stepfather? Thomas Henry Mayfield was
not mentioned in the rose-colored notebook.

Following clues in the notebook, Cox went to Cambridge to
track down the burial place of Ida's brother Louis, who had
died by drowning there in 1865. He finally found an old headstone, half buried, on which the inscription read: "Erected
by Ann Walsh in memory of her husband Thomas Walsh who
died in San Francisco in 1864"; other children who had died
in infancy were listed, then Louis Walsh, died May 21, 1865,
age 13 years. Thomas Walsh was the man Ida had referred to
in her notebook as "Father." Then it was clear that Ann Walsh,
who had put up the headstone, was Ida's mother. This confirmed that Ida must have been a Walsh. A Margaret Walsh
named on the headstone could very well be Thomas's mother.

While in Cambridge, Cox also tracked down an old neighbor
of the Walshes who remembered the family. She remembered
the crippled baby of the family, Emma, being visited and
given pretty clothes by Ellen Harvey (a name Ida had used in
buying a house in New York). Cox located grandmother Margaret Walsh's home and found she had deeded it before her
death to her son Thomas, Ida's father, and in 1862, on the
eve of his departure to California, he had sold it to his daughter
Mary, Ida's sister. It was after the death of young Louis that
Mary sold the house and came with her mother to New York
to live, and there the Walshes were transformed, for ununder-
standable reasons, into Mayfields. By 1872 Ida's mother Ann
Mary Walsh, widow of Thomas, had become Mary E. Mayfield, widow of an imaginary Henry Mayfield, New Orleans
sugar planter; her daughter Mary had become Mary E. Mayfield, and her son Michael had become Henry Mayfield.

During her reminiscences to the nurses during her last days,
Ida had often mentioned Patrick Crawford, her mother's father, who was a Dublin baker and often gave bread to the

poor; and she talked about a pair of Crawford cousins, children of her Uncle Patrick, who had been left in the care of her "Aunt Eliza in Salem, Massachusetts."

Through an ad in a Boston newspaper, Cox found a woman named Katherine Sheehan, who identified a picture Cox took along as her grandmother—the Aunt Eliza that Ida had spoken of. Eliza was Ann Mary Walsh's sister, Eliza Crawford O'Connor. That bakery was an important link. Ida had talked about it, and in Eliza Crawford O'Connor's family the bakery was a living tradition, according to Mrs. Sheehan. Eliza was the daughter of Patrick Crawford, who had owned the bakery. Cox immediately went off to Ireland to check on Mrs. Sheehan's story about Eliza, and to find clues pointing to Ida's Irish family connections. There he learned that Patrick Crawford *had* owned a bakery in Dublin at the time of the bread riots. Among the birth, death, and marriage records, Cox also found that Patrick Crawford, a baker of Bow Lane, had married Ann Crawford. Those two were Ida's maternal grandparents. They had five children: Ann, born in Dublin, who married Thomas Walsh; Eliza, Mary, and Margaret, all Ida's aunts; and Patrick, her uncle.

Cox's inquiries also brought out the information that Eliza had been cast out by her father because she became a Catholic, had gone to England, and had gotten married there to Thomas O'Connor. Wherever Eliza went, her sister Ann was sure to follow, so Cox went to England to pick up the trail of Ida's identity. It turned out that Ann did follow Eliza to England, met a friend of O'Connor's named Thomas Walsh, a hawker of textiles, and married him in Manchester in 1836. Their first child was a son. The second was a daughter, baptized Ellen Walsh. Ellen took on the name of Ida later, when she invented a new life for herself in America as Ida Mayfield, taking her family with her into the grand deception that she practiced her whole life as the wife of Benjamin Wood. The birth records of all the children born to the Walshes had all been recorded in that yellowed memorandum Cox had found among Ida's effects and had been unable to decipher at the time, as only abbreviations of the names and places had been used.

By 1845 both the O'Connors and the Walshes were established in Massachusetts: the Walshes in Boston and the O'Connors in Salem. Things went badly for both men, financially and otherwise. O'Connor died in a fire, and Walsh went to California to look for work and died.

Cox finally thought he had enough evidence on Ida's identity. The case began in August 1937. Originally about 200 people had claimed relationship. By now 1,103 persons had filed notices of claimed relationship. Of this number, 616 appeared in court to press their claims, accompanied by their lawyers. The counsel table was too small to accommodate all the attorneys present, and many had to sit on chairs usually reserved for prospective witnesses or for the public. The first trial was to determine who was closest to Ida through her husband. The Blanche Wood Shields faction was composed of the children and grandchildren of Ben's son Henry. The surrogate ruled that the five Wood descendants Gertrude, Henry, Howard S. Wood, Blanche Wood Shields, and Mabel Wood Russ were the nearest and next of kin to Ben Wood as his direct descendants. By this decision alone, the court eliminated 75 Wood claimants more remotely related to Ben. The five Woods who remained would be entitled to Ida's estate only if it were determined that she had left no blood relations.

The next issue was proof of Ida's identity through her parents, the establishment of her maiden name, and the determination of whether she had left any blood relatives. In presenting his case that Ida was a Walsh, not a Mayfield, Cox was not acting as attorney for any claimant to her fortune. He was neutral, reporting the results of his investigation as counsel to the public administrator. He presented all the birth, death, marriage, etc., documents he had gathered through the years in America and abroad to establish his claim that Ida was Ellen Walsh, the daughter of Thomas and Ann Crawford Walsh, the maternal granddaughter of Patrick and Ann Crawford. Cox's documentary evidence was overwhelming.

Next came the Mayfields with their claims. The courtroom was thick with southern accents and shoeless people. They tried to prove that Ida was the daughter of Thomas Henry Mayfield and Mary Ann Crawford of St. Tammany Parish, Louisiana, near New Orleans, had grown up on the old plantation, had met Ben Wood in Louisiana while Ben was working there as a gatherer of Spanish moss, gotten into trouble with him, came north with him to live as his wife, had the child Emma before their marriage, and eventually married him in 1867. At least they all agreed on the marriage date. They averred that a family in Malden, Massachusetts, named Walsh had befriended Ida, moved in with her later when Mr. Walsh died, and that Ida embraced the Walsh daughter as a sister and Ann Mary Walsh as her mother. The Walshes in turn had adopted Ida's name of Mayfield. That was their story. None of the witnesses had any documentary proof of their claims or of Ida's having been in Louisiana, as compared to the mass of documentary evidence produced by Cox. Judge Foley's decision was that Ida Wood was born Ellen Walsh, daughter of Thomas Walsh and Ann Crawford Walsh. He pointed out Ida's penchant for secrecy, her frequent changes of names, and her pretensions to a position in society that made her change her and her family's name from Walsh to the more elegant-sounding Mayfield. No appeal was taken on the decision.

Of course, the case didn't end there. It took two years of intensive investigation to determine the heirs of Ida who were alive when she died. Only those heirs who survived her were entitled to the inheritance. On May 17, 1937, Surrogate Foley announced the names of the ten persons who shared equally in Ida's fortune, each of them first cousins once removed and thereby within the fifth degree of kindred. Six were the grandchildren of Ida's Aunt Eliza. Three of these were the children of Aunt Eliza's daughter Eliza Jane, two were the children of Eliza's daughter Winifred, and the sixth was the son of Eliza's daughter Emmaline. Three were the grandchildren of Ida's Aunt Mary, who had married the foreman in grandfather Patrick Crawford's Dublin bakery. The tenth was the grandson of Ida's Uncle Patrick. None of those who inherited Ida's fortune had ever met Ida or even knew of her existence except for Mrs. Sheehan, the one who had answered the Boston ad and identified the picture Cox had shown her as her grandmother—the Aunt Eliza that Ida had often spoken of.

Joseph A. Cox, counsel to the public administrator, whose tireless search revealed the true identity of Ida Wood, resulting in the right heirs receiving her fortune, wrote a book about the case called *The Recluse of Herald Square,* a thoroughly fascinating book that proved that truth is stranger than fiction. Even after the case ended, Cox kept trying to reconstruct the great hoax, Ida's deception, which became her life. Poverty and trouble had been the dominant themes in Ida's life in her early formative years at home, which gave her a sense of insecurity and anxiety over the troubles and violence in Ireland that she constantly heard about. Cox felt there was reason to believe Ida went into domestic service at the age of twelve, after the family moved to Boston. She worked for a rich family named Johnson, and the young Johnson son, named Harvey, fell for her and tried to educate her to a new station in life, to culture. There Ellen (Ida) ripened from a gawky twelve-year-old into a beautiful nineteen-year-old woman. A possible theory is that Emma was Ida's child by Harvey, as she was born in 1857, the year Ida appeared in New York. This theory would account for Ida's anxiety to take Emma into her own family and pass her off as Ben Wood's child. Ida called herself Mrs. Harvey during those early years in New York, and even bought a house under the name of Ida Harvey, at which point she began to think of herself as Ida, not Ellen. She heard about rich Ben Wood from a friend and wrote him the letter that led to their getting together. During her years as a rich socialite she had made no close friends, probably for fear that her true origin and identity might be discovered. This fear finally drove her into complete withdrawal as a recluse.

Chapter 4
Everybody's Dream

The dream of waking up and finding that a distant relative has left you a fortune came true in ten homes scattered across the land when the will of Mrs. Sylvia Ann Howland Green Wilks was filed after her death at the age of eighty in New York in 1951. Mrs. Wilks left close to $100 million, the bulk of which went to sixty-three charities, churches, and educational institutions in all parts of the United States, with many of which she had no previous connection whatsoever.

Mrs. Wilks' original will was written in 1925; a codicil was added in 1928, and another in 1948. The 1928 codicil was found in a cabinet with four bars of soap. The others turned up in safe deposit boxes. Just which of the wills named the ten distant relatives, who received $100,000 each, is not known. What is known is that Mrs. Wilks hired a genealogist to track down all the descendants of Gideon Howland, her forebear who started the family fortune in the whaling business in New Bedford, Massachusetts. The amazing thing is that though she tracked them down and named them in her will, she made no effort to contact them.

Mrs. Elsie H. Leicester of San Francisco was incredulous when she heard of her windfall. She had never heard of Mrs. Wilks. Leonard B. Almy of Keystone, Oklahoma, was thunderstruck. "Now I can own a farm of my own," he said. Herman Loomis, eighty-four, of Rochester, New York, never saw Mrs. Wilks and was not sure of his relationship to her, but said he was too old to enjoy the bequest anyhow. Lina Eppendorff, of Poughkeepsie, died a month before Mrs. Wilks, but her own heirs did not benefit from her $100,000 bequest—it reverted to the Wilks estate. Mrs. Sylvia Geib, seventy-six, lived on a farm near Buffalo, Missouri, when she heard of her bequest and didn't plan to change her mode of life and start taking things easy "until she got old." Perhaps the least surprised legatee was Dr. Robert Walker, who lived in New Bedford and probably knew of the family connection.

An interesting bequest was that of $10,000 to William M. Emery, a genealogist and retired newspaperman. He was undoubtedly the one who tracked down all those distant relatives. Another specific bequest was $12,000 to Bert Hill of South Dartmouth, who was superintendent for many years of Mrs. Wilks' estate "Round Hill."

The will was contested by Mrs. Emilie Keene Elmendorf Colles of White Plains, New York, a cousin, who received $5,000 under the will, and by the Girl Scouts of America, cut off from a legacy in an earlier will. A settlement was reached nine months after Mrs. Wilks' death, with Mrs. Colles receiving $140,000 tax free, and the Girl Scouts of America receiving $50,000. Incidentally, all the bequests were tax free, the estate paying the tax on all the legacies.

What kind of a woman was Mrs. Wilks? She was tall, austere, lonely, and a miser, her only pleasure being the possession of and the building up of the fortune left her by her mother Hetty Green. Hetty Green was known as the richest woman in the world and commonly referred to as "the wizard of Wall Street" before her death in 1916. Through ironclad provisions in her will she was able to prevent a breakup of her fortune for thirty-five years after her death. She had left her entire estate of $125 million to her two children, Sylvia Wilks and Colonel Edward H. R. Green, with the proviso that the surviving child should inherit from the other. Colonel Green died before his sister, and obediently willed $43 million to Sylvia. His widow received only $500,000 of her husband's estate, and waged a long court battle to get that much.

Hetty Green imposed a childhood of poverty on her two children. In fact, her son lost a leg due to his mother's unwillingness to pay for proper medical care. When Edward injured his knee while coasting, Hetty disguised herself as a beggar and took him to a charity hospital. When the leg finally had to be amputated, Hetty had the operation performed in a boarding house. A familiar sight in Bellows Falls, Vermont, where they lived at the time, was young Sylvia pulling her crippled older brother around in a cart. When the family moved from there to Hoboken, New Jersey, they lived in a squalid rooming house, even though Hetty was a multimillionairess at the time.

Sylvia was thirty-eight when she married Matthew Astor Wilks, then sixty-seven, a wealthy grandson of John Jacob Astor. Wilks left Sylvia $1 million when he died in 1926. From then on Sylvia lived in seclusion, practically her only contact being her brother, Colonel Green. Unlike Sylvia, Colonel Green was amiable, loved meeting people, and opened his estate to the public during his lifetime. Sylvia was miserly, like her mother, but Colonel Green spent money freely, and had a carefree life indeed, despite his handicap of the lost leg.

Those ten surprised inheritors of $100,000 each certainly didn't consider Sylvia Wilks miserly. But since they were all quite elderly when they received their bequests, they might have wished that Mrs. Wilks had seen fit to send it along sooner.

Chapter 5

No Garden of Roses

Showman Billy Rose was not noted for keeping his cool, but was forced to cool it, for nearly two years after his death, in a cold-storage receiving vault while his two sisters wrangled with the executors of his estate over the cost of his mausoleum and tangled with the courts in their efforts to break his will. Billy would have been the first, and possibly the only one, to see the humor of his lying above ground for nearly two years wearing the ghastly ruby lips and thick black eyebrows Jamaican undertakers are prone to apply to their customers. Dying at all would have been his first regret, but dying on the island of Jamaica, where he had a home, would have been a close second.

By the time he was finally buried, Billy would have been happy to have *any* resting place. His first choice would have been to be laid to rest amidst the $1 million worth of sculpture that he presented to the National Museum of Israel in Jerusalem, but unfortunately the Israeli government decided a museum should not be used for a burial ground. Some people think that the futuristic sculpture Billy donated to Israel was frightening enough in itself. George Jessel wandered through the Billy Rose Garden of Sculpture in Jerusalem one day, becoming more and more bewildered as he looked at the unrecognizable shapes. But when he came to a misshapen piece of rock painted red and white and labeled "Mother and Child," Jessel exclaimed, "What did Billy have against Israel?"

Billy always was a conversation piece, both in life and in death. He wasn't particularly well loved, but he was always spectacular. Born in a Lower East side tenement in 1899, he went on to successful careers as the fastest stenographer in the world, a songwriter, nightclub impresario, theatrical producer, real estate operator, investor, and lover. In that last category, Billy had four wives, one of whom he married twice, and numerous well-publicized romances in between. His divorce from his first wife, Fannie Brice, made international headlines. His divorce from his second wife, Eleanor Holm, cost him over a quarter of a million dollars. His marriage to Doris Vidor only lasted six months. His fourth and fifth wives, because he married and divorced her twice, were Joyce Matthews. Apparently Billy didn't put much faith in the permanence of any of his marriages, as evidenced by the fact that he never actually *gave* any of his wives the beautiful jewelry he liked to see them wear. He loaned it to them.

Billy made it big, financially. Under the able tutelage of Bernard Baruch, who took him on as a personal secretary, Billy learned about finances and investing, and at the time of his death was the largest individual holder of American Telephone & Telegraph stock as well as innumerable other securities. Among his other holdings were the Ziegfeld and Billy Rose theaters, a large residence at 56 East 93rd Street, and other residences at Tavern Island; Norwalk, Connecticut; and Montego Bay, Jamaica (where he had gone to recuperate from an operation when he died). The value of the estate was estimated at between $25 million and $30 million.

Billy probably thought he made a very sensible and forthright will. His two sisters didn't think so. He left most of his estate to a charitable foundation bearing his own name, and left seventeen specific bequests amounting to $175,000. Among these were a bequest of $10,000 to Eleanor Holm, which was made in a codicil to the will dated February 7, 1966, three days before he died. This was done when Billy received forty dollars worth of stone crabs (his favorite delicacy) sent him from Miami by Eleanor when she heard he was ill. Billy also left $50,000 and the income from a $1 million trust to Joyce Matthews (who had remarried in the meantime). To Joyce's daughter, Victoria Berlinger (adopted when Joyce was married to Milton Berle), Rose left $10,000 and the income from a $100,000 trust. He also established a $100,000 trust for a sister, Mrs. Miriam Stern of New York. His other sister, Mrs. Polly Gottlieb of Beverly Hills, was left $50,000 and the income of a $1 million trust. The principal of all the trusts reverts to the Billy Rose Foundation on the death of the beneficiaries.

The two sisters sued to have the will nullified and to get themselves declared sole heirs of the estate, asserting that the Billy Rose Foundation, organized in 1958, had never done much charity work. They lost their suit, and the will leaving the bulk of his estate to Billy's foundation was upheld.

It was a hassle over the cost of the mausoleum that kept little Billy above ground so long after he died. The sisters chose the biggest plot in the Westchester Hills Cemetery in Ardsley, New York, which cost $48,000, and planned a monument designed by sculptor Isamu Noguchi. The executors of the estate disagreed with the sisters over the amount to be spent, and demanded written notice from the sisters that they would indemnify the executors should the courts rule that the sum spent for burial was more than "a reasonable amount." That really riled them. It was finally agreed that the mausoleum should cost $60,000 and that the plot (large enough to accommodate eighty average-size graves) could cost $45,000. Perpetual care was also granted. That should make up for all those months in a cold-storage vault!

Chapter 6
Reigning Cats and Dogs

Probably the largest single group of willmakers who leave unusual bequests are pet lovers. Dogs and cats come in for the largest share of these bequests, but parrots, canaries, a dove, and even a donkey have lived like kings after the death of their masters.

The largest such bequest was that of Eleanor E. Ritchey, heiress to the Quaker State Refining Corporation, who died in Fort Lauderdale in 1968, leaving her entire estate, then worth $4.5 million, to her 150 stray dogs. By the time the will had been contested by relatives and was finally settled in September of 1973, the assets of the estate had grown to $14 million, and only 73 of the 150 dogs were still living.

In the final settlement, the dogs were awarded $9 million, about $123,287 each, in a trust fund, and $2 million was divided among half sisters Marion Boyer and Lois Leavy and half brother John Ritchey, all from Pennsylvania. The rest of the estate went for taxes and attorneys' and executors' fees. Circuit Judge Leroy Moe said one of the larger problems in settling the affair was determining the value of the dogs. It was finally decided that all of them were valued at $1.

Tattooed to prove their membership in the original 150, the dogs were separated by sex so as to prevent propagation. Accidental offspring would be eligible to receive benefits from the estate (what, through a wire fence?). Originally the bequest was to stay in effect until the last dog is dead, or for a maximum of 20 years, after which the estate was to pass on to the Auburn Research Foundation at Auburn University in Alabama, for study of diseases of small animals. Apparently that stipulation still holds.

Approximately $17,000 is spent each year on the dogs' food and housing, while another $12,000 per year pays for their weekly medical checkups and treatment of illnesses.

Mrs. Andree O. Montet, a childless widow of Charlotte, North Carolina, left her $250,000 estate to her two canaries and her tomcat Tommie. One of the canary heiresses, named Gigi, was found dead, and foul play on the part of Tommie was suspected. The attorney for the estate ordered a postmortem on Gigi and put a close watch on the other canary, Co-Co, to prevent Tommie's becoming the sole heir. Things were pretty tense until the postmortem revealed Gigi had died a natural death, and Tommie was exonerated.

Toots, a registered Siamese cat, changed her eating habits after her mistress Mrs. Hazel Kurrur Mathein left $50,000, including her home and her blue-chip stocks, for the care of the cat. Her guardian, who received free rent in the house in return for caring for Toots, made the mistake of starting to cook for the cat rather than giving it cat food. Now Toots turns up her nose at chicken, preferring ocean perch and salmon. All those relatives who will come into the estate after Toots passes on, would probably like to add an item or two to that diet.

Allen Foster, of Little Rock, Arkansas, was really hard up for companionship. For more than two years before his death his only friend was a large Rhode Island Red hen. Foster willed that after his death the hen should be maintained in the manner to which she had become accustomed. The local legend is that the hen became so arrogant after becoming an heiress that she was ostracized by her barnyard companions and died a lonesome death at an advanced age.

One fat cat got so upset over all the hoopla following his inheritance that he became a nervous wreck and died within a year. His master, Woodbury Rand, left Buster, his eight-year-old tiger cat, $100,000, but subsequent legal hassles cut him down to $40,000. Buster just couldn't take all those newsreel and press photographers hanging around, and surrendered the last of his nine lives. Buster's caretaker got what was left of the estate for her faithfulness.

Lucius Beebe's huge St. Bernard named T-Bone Towser didn't inherit as big an estate as he might have expected from his loving master. He only received a $15,000 trust fund so he could be maintained in comfort for the remainder of his natural life. But T-Bone got a fringe benefit few dogs get. He was allowed free use of Beebe's elegant private railroad car called "Virginia City." As a matter of fact, it was largely for T-Bone's benefit that Beebe bought the private railway car in the first place—he wanted to take T-Bone with him wherever he went, and regular trains were not enthusiastic over the dog's presence. At that, T-Bone did better than Beebe's six nieces and nephews—they only got $1,000 each.

One old tomcat named Casey didn't appreciate being left everything by his master Morton Shirks, a railroad conductor, and absconded. And Shirks had gone to such pains to ensure Casey's comfort, too—he'd not only left his home and everything in it to Casey, but had also stipulated that the furniture was not to be rearranged by any human tenants because the shift might confuse his pet. Casey's disappearance threw the case into court, as the relatives next in line after him wanted to sell the house. A county judge finally judged Casey to be dead and authorized the sale of the house.

A cat named Tibber got rid of her sordid financial worries when she was left $1,400 by her English master William Butler "because she served as a watchdog each night when he went out for a drink."

A talking dog named Tiger, of Ogden, Utah, didn't talk fast enough when he tried to muscle into a share of the $6 million that animal lover George Whittell bequeathed for the care and feeding of orphaned pets. Tiger put in his plea by way of his master, Kenneth Owens, who wanted $20,000 with which to take Tiger on tour displaying his vocal skills. It turned out Tiger only had two phrases in his vocabulary: "I want out" and "I want some." Well, if you can only say two things, those two would serve many a purpose.

A gray mongrel named Mac and his pal George, a half-breed cocker spaniel, really put on the dog when their master, Thomas Shewbridge, a prune rancher of California, left them an estate worth $112,000 in 1958. The estate was turned into twenty-nine thousand shares of San Jose Water Works common stock, and the dogs' favorite outing was when they attended a water works board of directors session.

A poodle named Jill and a spaniel named Donna know what it is to go from riches to rags. These two survivors of a once-substantial four-dog family are broke after using up a $15,000 inheritance. When Mrs. Emily Storrow of Pasadena left the bequest, she provided the money should last ten years—the dogs' life expectancy. Two of the heirs succumbed on schedule, but old Jill and Donna hung in there. The Humane Society, which took care of them when they were rich, took pity on their penniless senior citizens and let them stay on. But the steaks didn't come quite so often after that.

A great many animals benefited from the will of Elsie Ferguson, a stage and screen star of the 1920s. She left $500,000 to the Animal Medical Center in Manhattan when she died in 1961. Also included in her will were bequests to the Bide-a-Wee Home, Orphans of the Storm, the American Society for the Prevention of Cruelty to Animals, and the Royal Society for the Prevention of Cruelty to Animals in England.

The Royal Society for the Prevention of Cruelty to Animals in England probably doesn't come into many bequests such as Miss Ferguson's from America, but it does very well in English wills. The present annual total received in bequests is about $4.8 million. The society honored the bequest of one woman who wanted the money used to feed the pigeons on South London's Wimbledon Common. They also cared for a donkey left to them with money for its upkeep.

In leaving her $1 million estate for a home for friendless animals, Lillian Schaaf specified that only lovers of animals could be employed at the animal shelter, built on property she owned near Worthington, Ohio. This will was a surprise, as Mrs. Schaaf hadn't had a pet for twenty years.

Even a dove came into an inheritance of $1,500 from its owner, Edna Schopper. We have yet to unearth a will leaving anything to a giraffe, kangaroo, or ostrich.

Chapter 7

  Dime Store Dynasty

Woolworth's is a household word, an institution, a name three
generations have known and loved because of the wondrous
array of bargains to be found there. Though Woolworth's has
long since ceased being a five-and-ten-cent store, the memory
of those good old days lingers on, and we still say we're going
to the five-and-ten-cent store . . . and we mean Woolworth's.
That red sign with the gold lettering is as familiar to us as the
face of our oldest friend. Songs, movies, and books have been
written about it. We've all read reams of newspaper publicity
about some of the people whose fortunes came from Woolworth's, particularly Barbara Hutton and the Donahue brothers, Jimmy and "Wooly."

But how many of us know how it all started, the trials and
tribulations of the families involved, and how the money we
spent at Woolworth's was handled and disbursed by them?
Among the books written on the subject, the most interesting were a biography of Barbara Hutton by Dean Jennings
and *Five and Ten* by John K. Winkler. A summary of the
story of the Woolworths, culled from these books, conversations with Woolworth executives, and reading the wills of
members of the family, will give you an idea of the fascinating
history of that name we all take for granted in our lives—Woolworth.

A farm-born man named Frank Winfield Woolworth started
it all, in the latter part of the nineteenth century.

Anyone knowing Frank Woolworth for the first twenty-
eight years of his life would have been sure to say he was a
"born loser." He even thought so himself.

Born on a farm in Jefferson County, New York, his first twenty-one years were spent helping his only brother, Charles Sumner, with the chores during long, cold winters and dusty, hot summers. All of which they hated.

With dreams of having a store of his own one day, Frank went to Watertown, where he worked in a small dry-goods store for nothing, to gain experience.

For the next six years he worked endlessly, selling, sweeping floors, washing windows, and delivering packages. The highest salary he ever received was ten dollars a week, and that only lasted a short time, as he still was a bad salesman.

It was during his ten-dollar "prosperity" that he proposed to Jennie Creighton, a beautiful girl who made her living making hats.

With great love and courage, even though jobless and penniless, they married, signed a three-hundred-dollar note, took a six-hundred-dollar mortgage, and bought a four-acre farm. They raised chickens which gave Frank a distaste for chicken in any form for the rest of his life.

Four months later Frank was offered a job by a former employer who liked the way he trimmed windows. The salary was ten dollars.

It took Jennie a year to dispose of the farm. In the meanwhile, with Frank only able to come home one night a week, it was lonely. The offer to buy the farm came just in time. Jennie was expecting a baby.

Hearing of five-cent counters in dry-goods stores, Frank was so excited by the concept that he secured a loan of three hundred dollars' worth of merchandise to start his own store. It failed in two months.

Having a taste of owning his own store, Frank tried again in another location and added ten-cent items for more variety.

This store was such a success he sent for his brother to open another. It failed. He tried again. Another failure.

Having unswerving determination and belief, he tried again in Scranton and brought in his second successful store. Oddly enough, it was due to a glib salesman practically wishing

Christmas tree ornaments on him, which Frank didn't like, that made the store a success.

And so his luck turned. By the end of 1880, Frank had repaid all his debts and had two thousand dollars saved. He took Jennie back to Watertown for a triumphant homecoming. His many friends gathered around, asking that he save jobs for them as new stores opened. The mother of his third cousins, Fred and Herbert Woolworth, asked him to save jobs for her sons when they grew up.

Doing all his own buying, Frank took a desk room in New York City, thereby laying the foundation of what was to become the largest retail buying organization in the world.

In 1889 Frank met B. H. Hunt, buyer for Horace Partridge & Company, who told him how much cheaper toys could be purchased in Europe. Frank sailed with Hunt. It was Frank's first trip abroad.

Writing back frequently, Frank commented from England: "Think a good penny and sixpence store would be a sensation if run by a real live 'Yankee.'" He added, "Though it is almost impossible to understand Englishmen, they talk so different from us, and they have hard work to understand us sometimes." He noted with surprise that "Dress suits for Gents is the rule," and with a bit of a shock, "Ladies wear very low neck dresses in all public places." Frank went to Germany for dolls and Christmas tree ornaments made by women and children who were paid a penny a piece for their labor. To Frank's horror, "Everyone speaks Dutch!" After visiting the Summer Palace of the Emperor Napoleon, Napoleonic decor was to have considerable influence on Frank thereafter.

As the great tide of immigration set in, Frank kept elaborate charts and placed his stores accordingly. With sales well over a million dollars a year, Frank was able to have a summer home on the Jersey shore and a thirty-room mansion on Fifth Avenue filled with French furniture, red-and-gold paneling, and luxurious rugs. Indulging his love of music to the fullest, he had installed an automatic organ in oak and gold. Frank worked out a number of ingenious mechanical devices such as concealed colored lights. By pressing a button, the room could be thrown into pitch darkness. Another button and a symphony would commence, the lights changing to follow the mood of the music, from amber to green to mauve. Also by pressing a button, a large oil portrait of the composer would appear in a panel at the top. The famous Hungarian artist Joannes de Tahy painted the portraits. Finally sound effects were added: thunder, lightning, rain. These were so lifelike that women frequently clutched their coiffures.

From this mansion his daughter Helena was married to Charles McCann, and his daughter Edna to Franklyn Laws Hutton, a young, socially prominent stockbroker. Later his daughter Jessie married James Paul Donahue, a handsome Irish American whose father supported a large family rendering fats and hides. She had met him at a skating rink. Father Frank was only lukewarm about the marriage.

Due to overwork, Frank had a bout of ill health and decided to incorporate in order to protect his many thousands of employees. He did this in his own way, with the stock being held by himself, managers, and employees.

In 1909, doing a business of twenty million dollars a year, Frank decided the time was ripe to open a chain in England. His executives were all against it. Not wishing to uproot any of them against their wishes, he called for volunteers to be store managers. Three responded, among them his third cousin, Fred Woolworth.

The first store did a nice but not overwhelming business. The second was opened soon after; the English people were familiar enough with the penny-and-sixpence bargains to create a riot, and the police had to stem the crowds. By 1912 there were twenty-eight English Woolworth stores, and all but two were managed by Englishmen, whom Frank discovered could do as well as a "Yankee." The early volunteers became executives and directors. Fred became managing director.

On the "home front" Fred's brother, Herbert Woolworth, who had gone to work for Frank's brother, decided to go it alone by forming a five-million-dollar corporation with unfriendly rivals of Frank. But the corporation's use of the same storefronts, plus the name of Woolworth, so incensed Frank that he took matters into his own hands.

Each night after his rivals had trimmed their own windows for the following day, Frank and his employees scouted the windows, returning to their own stores at wee hours in the morning. Frank had all his windows trimmed with identical merchandise, but at half the price. When the competition countered by reducing theirs, Frank again lowered.

Frank, who made millionaires of over one hundred men, watched as the men who tried to thwart him went down like kingpins, Herbert Woolworth & Company included.

Frank now decided to push through another dream of his: building the tallest office building in the world. In 1913, when the edifice was completed, he gave a banquet. The lights were lowered and the recently inaugurated President of the United States, Woodrow Wilson, pressed a button in Washington, which lit eighty thousand electric light bulbs. It was the proudest moment of Frank's sixty-one years.

In 1916, with an income of over two million dollars a year, he ordered to be built a Renaissance palace of white marble of unsurpassing splendor in Glen Cove.

After Frank's years of success and happiness, the year 1918 brought tragedy. His daughter Edna was found dead in her hotel room at the Savoy Hotel in New York City, where she was staying temporarily. She left a husband and an only daughter, Barbara, then ten years old. Barbara would one day make front-page news with her wealth and seven marriages. Later that year, his granddaughter, eight-year-old Gladys Helena McCann, also died.

But an even greater tragedy had been intruding on Frank's life. His beloved Jennie had been more and more regressing into the past. That year he was forced to have her legally declared mentally incompetent.

Frank's health began to fail. He had a close friend who died soon after having his teeth extracted, and this scared Frank of ever going to a dentist. His teeth got so bad he could only eat soft foods. He later developed gallstones and uremic poisoning, lapsed into unconsciousness, and died a few days before turning sixty-seven.

He left a hand-written will in large Spencerian script, made just prior to his first trip abroad, on July 31, 1889. In it he left everything he possessed to Jennie, trusting her to make provisions for the children. She was named executrix without bond. The estate was valued at twenty-seven million dollars, after deducting eight million dollars for taxes.

Jennie was never aware of the death of her daughter and grandchild. She lived in a world where all her children were babies again. It can truly be said that Jennie gave her life to Frank and his stores, which she loved. While she still knew they all needed her, she maintained her strength and helped in every way she could.

Nor was she seemingly aware of Frank's passing. He was still the handsome young stalwart, who had wooed and won her, the father of her babies. Even less was she aware of the millions spilling into her hands, like falling autumn leaves.

Frank had been thinking of changing his will for some years. Leaving enough for Jennie to continue living and being taken care of in the style to which she was accustomed, he intended to leave the rest of his wealth to his two daughters and to Barbara, the daughter of Edna, plus trust funds for his other grandchildren.

Frank changed and rechanged the wording of his will over a period of years, but never signed his name to any of the revised wills. It is impossible to discover why Frank had never done this, since he was too intelligent not to realize that chaos would ensue, and his lawyers had warned him. So one can only conjecture that each time he took pen in hand, he recalled the many beautiful days of long ago, when they worked so hard and were so happy—the days when he and his first and only love, Jennie, exchanged their little wills together, having very little to will, but willing it to each other. But the fact remains that he did not sign a new will, and the secret of why is locked in his heart forever.

Jennie outlived her husband by five years. The will Jennie had written when Frank wrote his was an exact duplicate, except that she left everything to Frank. Since Frank was dead, Jennie's will was totally invalid and her huge estate had to be probated by the courts, and business administration papers took the place of a will. What took Frank and Jennie a little over a page to write, took several hundred pages and about six years to consummate.

Due to F.W. not having left a will when he died, which would have distributed the estate to his heirs with only the first tax, the estate was retaxed on Jennie's death for an extra state tax of $1.9 million and a federal tax of $13 million. The estate came to $60 million, exclusive of property. The Woolworth building was sold to pay the taxes. Ninety thousand shares of Woolworth stock were distributed immediately. A short time later an additional 405,000 shares were distributed. Stock was still being distributed in 1930.

The courts distributed the estate three ways: to Helena McCann; Jessie Donahue; and Barbara Hutton, sole issue of the deceased daughter, Edna Hutton. At that time, Barbara was eleven years old, residing with her father, Franklyn Hutton. Franklyn was named her guardian and George Hutton, her special guardian.

According to the reports Franklyn was obliged to send to the courts, Barbara's worth was increased by $25 million in one year, nine months, due to his wise investments. By 1930, the value of Barbara's estate was $86.4 million.

There is no record as to the increase of the other estates, since they were not obliged to report to the court.

Daughter Jessie Woolworth, a tall, willowy blonde with a lyric soprano voice of operatic quality, had a disposition her friends described as "saintly." A friend in need could always count on her help. She married a handsome Irishman named James Paul Donahue, with whom she was madly in love. She lavished on him such gifts as a private Pullman car worth $50 thousand, and then, using the letters of his name, she christened it "Japauldon." She presented him with "Wooldon

Manor," a big estate in Southampton, Long Island, and a $2 million estate, "Cielito Lindo," in Palm Beach. She also maintained the house at 6 East 80th Street, New York City.

She provided him with large sums for gambling, which he loved; but then, so did Jessie. It was reported by the society columnist, Suzy, that Jessie put aside $250 thousand a year to gamble at chemin de fer at Monte Carlo and other European resorts.

According to Dean Jennings, "with no work in sight," James took up crap shooting, roulette, baccarat and other nocturnal skills with such enthusiasm that Jessie was forced to budget his losses. "From now on, darling," she reproved him, "you may not lose more than twenty-five thousand dollars a night."

Having come from a relatively poor family, James was constantly amazed by the grandeur of things he didn't understand. Again, according to Dean Jennings, James once asked a neighbor to inspect his dining room, saying: "Come and see it. All the silver's gold!"

On another occasion, Donahue decorated his private ballroom with white orchids for a dinner dance at which the famous Webb quartet was hired to play. He met the musicians at the door and in astonishment asked, "Are there only *four* of you?"

Jessie's jewels were fabulous: diamonds, emeralds, and sapphires, though her $600 thousand rope of Oriental pearls was her favorite.

And so they lived in opulent splendor. Their children loved their mother and adored their father, whom they followed in the business of doing nothing, but doing it in the grand manner.

The year 1929 wasn't such a good one for Jessie as far as her jewels were concerned. Two or three of her prize gems were stolen. This didn't mean a lot to Jessie, as she was as wont to wear jewels from Woolworth's five and tens as not; and besides, they were insured. She was very distressed, however, when the pearls were missing. But all of this paled into insignificance when she suddenly lost the prize jewel of her whole life: her husband.

On April 19, 1931, the husband Jessie adored committed suicide by swallowing forty-five grains of bichloride of mercury. He died in agony, in the same sanitarium where Jessie, beside herself with shock and horror, was being treated for a nervous breakdown. It was rumored at the time that he was being blackmailed by persons with homosexual photographs at their disposal.

Jessie closed the house on 80th Street and never set foot in it again. She gave up her house in Palm Beach, and whenever she returned for a visit with friends, she stayed at the Everglades Club. No longer did she attend parties, but was content to play bridge, of which she was very fond, and visit with her two sons.

She bought a twenty-eight-room triplex apartment at 834 Fifth Avenue in New York, where her son, Jimmy, stayed with her frequently. But tragedy was still to stalk her. In 1966, she lost Jimmy.

From then on, she never returned to Florida. If she went anywhere, it was to her Southampton home, where she had many bridge players. Her other son, Woolworth, known as "Wooly," came to see her frequently, particularly when he was staying at her Calverton lodge. And that was her life.

The last will and testament of Jessie Woolworth Donahue is dated November 21, 1968, and testifies to her generosity and goodness.

All debts owed to her were to be forgiven.

All amounts not fully paid up in her son Jimmy's will, due to lack of funds, were to be paid in full by her estate.

To her personal maid, Yvonne Francillon, Jessie's co-op apartment at 135 East 71st Street was to be deeded, complete with all furnishings, silverware, china, paintings, and all other property in it. She also willed Yvonne $100 thousand.

To her butler, Paul Steindl, $50 thousand.

To her secretary, Mary Bodner, $50 thousand.

To Virginia Ehret, $25 thousand.

To any other person in her employ for at least two years, $1 thousand for each full year of employment up to $10 thousand.

To her niece Barbara Hutton, the painting by Madame Vigée-Lebrun of Madame Lebrun's daughter Julie.

To her friend Dorland Doyle, the painting entitled "The Glasgow Royal Mail of the Road" by J. F. Herring.

To her son Woolworth, $100 thousand, plus the income from $1 million for as long as he lived, in addition to the use of the lodge and all effects of the lodge at Calverton, Long Island.

To Wooly's wife, Mary Hartline Donahue, her diamond ballet pin.

To Southampton Hospital, $50 thousand.

To be sold and made part of her residuary estate: antique gold snuff boxes inherited from her son Jimmy; her home and all property in Southampton, including all furnishings, silver, paintings, and other effects; the co-op at 834 Fifth Avenue and all effects therein; and all jewelry.

She directed that her trustees and executors were to divide all proceeds into twenty equal shares, which were to be distributed as follows:

To the American Cancer Society, fifteen equal shares.

To the Salvation Army, two equal shares.

To the Lighthouse (New York Association for the Blind), two equal shares.

To the American Red Cross, one equal share.

At a gala auction at the Parke-Bernet Galleries, just the money from her jewelry and furnishings brought in somewhat between $2 million and $3 million.

It would be difficult to say exactly how much all this came to, but it would be safe to say: The nickels and dimes that had accrued to the Woolworths over the years were now being returned by the millions to the public from which it came.

A self-dubbed "clown prince," Jimmy Donahue, handsome and very wealthy, was probably just that.

Traveling in "jet set" society, with all the so-called "beauti-

ful people," he was a favorite of his cousin, Barbara Hutton.
She even took him along on two of her honeymoons. Marrying
fast and frequently, Barbara was evidently sure of some of the
things she could count on in her husbands, but not their sense
of humor. The husbands didn't think it all that funny.

There were times when Jimmy's humor took rather bizarre
turns. During World War I, through the Roaring Twenties,
and into the thirties, there was a famous dancing team known
as the "Dolly Sisters." The toast of two continents, they were
always show-stoppers in the Ziegfeld Follies.

Well-known in theatrical circles, Jimmy ran into Rosie Dolly
and her manager in Cannes one afternoon and invited them
to his apartment for dinner. Upon arriving, Jimmy opened the
door—stark naked! Rosie's manager caught her as she was
about to faint over the threshold.

At another time, at a New Year's Eve party in a penthouse
of the Hampshire House in New York City, Jimmy hid in a
closet until midnight. At the stroke of twelve, he burst forth
in a top hat—and that was it (though he did have a long curling
horn, which he blew vociferously).

Unfortunately for the debutantes of the era, this wealthy
bachelor was not for them. It was well known that for sexual
companionship Jimmy preferred the boys to the girls.

As Dean Jennings recorded in his book, *Barbara Hutton,* a
candid biography:

> During World War II, Daniel A. Doran, a widely-
> known private detective, was asked to investigate
> Jimmy's nocturnal play, and Doran's agents spent
> considerable time with prosecutors, police officers
> and others both in Florida and New York. Their re-
> ports, complete in every pornographical detail were
> unprintable.

Frequently traveling with a coterie of "close" friends, Jimmy
was a familiar figure at all the chic resorts, here and abroad.
On the beach at Waikiki, the bathers were often amused by

the sight of Jimmy striding along the beach with four or five friends, the friends always keeping three paces behind their leader, Jimmy.

He was well-known at many "gay" bars where he appeared in "drag." And what "drag." Beautiful gowns and outfits. Bejeweled, some of it real, some paste. His make-up, incongruous but meticulous.

Then, rather suddenly, Jimmy moved away from his favorite stamping grounds and bought the country estate of Alfred Gwynne Vanderbilt. He filled it with a fortune in paintings and rare antiques, part of which he had collected himself and some of which his mother had given him.

His mother was aware of his weaknesses; in fact, on many occasions she bailed him out of a tight situation, but he was the one she could count on when she was lonely, and she adored him. He frequently stayed in her triplex apartment on Fifth Avenue when he wished to spend a while in the city. Usually he brought a male companion.

Thus it was that in 1966, while staying in his mother's apartment with a male friend, at an early hour in the morning, that the friend called Jimmy's brother, Wooly, to tell him in hushed tones that Jimmy was dead.

Jessie took the news stoically. By this time she had become inured to pain and tragedy. Wooly at that time had been operated on for cancer of the throat.

Again quoting from Dean Jennings' book:

> There were no marks on the body, no gun or knife or empty poison vial. The news reports said he died of "visceral congestion." Dr. James Lindsay Luke, then associate medical examiner for the City of New York, ordered an autopsy and there were no further stories on the case.
>
> Dr. Luke eventually made this revelation:
> The final cause of death of Mr. Donahue, is acute alcohol and barbiturate poisoning, circumstances undetermined. In other words, we are not able to de-

termine the motivation behind the ingestion of the barbiturate (Seconal) although the amount recovered from Mr. Donahue's tissues was far in excess of a medicinal or therapeutic dose.

The conclusion is plain. Like father, like son, Jimmy Donahue committed suicide.

Jimmy was fifty-one years old.

Jimmy's will, written two years before his death, left his entire collection of snuff boxes to be divided between his mother and his cousin, Barbara Hutton.

His home in Brookville, and everything in it, to his mother, plus all jewelry and remaining effects.

To the Archbishopric of New York, $500 thousand.

To the New York Foundling Hospital, $250 thousand, as an endowment fund to be known as "The James Donahue Fund." The fund was to be invested by the board of managers and the income thereafter to be used for the general purposes of the hospital.

To the Metropolitan Opera Association, $100 thousand.

To the United Cerebral Palsy, $100 thousand.

To his former governess, Mrs. Jeanne Olivier, $10 thousand, plus a life annuity of $6 thousand a year.

To Mary Bodner, an employee in his financial office, $5 thousand.

To all other employees who had been with him three or more years, $1 thousand, plus an additional $1 thousand to all for each year of employment, but not to exceed $10 thousand for any individual.

To one male friend, $200 thousand.

To two other male friends, $100 thousand apiece.

The residuary of the estate was willed to his brother, Woolworth.

To say that Wooly was born spoiled and never recovered would be an understatement.

He was asked to leave so many prep schools that there were

no more to go to. And always for the same reason: "Les girls." Wooly could find more ways of climbing out of windows or down fire escapes than the schools were able to cope with.

The nightclubs of the world recognized him with a smile whenever he entered. He became pals with royalty, famous matadors, and all the glamorous people. The walls of his trophy room became more and more crowded with the heads of animals he collected while on safari in Africa, India, or South America.

In 1940, he met and married Gretchen Wilson Hearst. This marriage ended in divorce in 1946.

Sixteen years passed before he tried the married state again, this time to Judith Johns. With her he had his only child, a daughter also named Judith—after which they were divorced.

Not long after, he met and married the real love of his life, the former Mary Hartline, a woman of considerable means herself. As a teen-ager, she starred in her own television series, portraying a glamorous but somewhat unlikely circus trainer. She was the idol of the Pablum set for many years.

Tragedy befell the marriage when Wooly had another operation for cancer of his throat. Mary, an accomplished cook despite eighteen servants, oversaw his special diet. She had a kitchen installed next to their bedroom suite so that Wooly, who was fond of midnight snacks, could have something she had prepared especially for him.

Their mansion on Via Bellaria Road in Palm Beach seemed so magnificent that one could hardly imagine anything more. But they could. Aside from a beach house, they bought an even bigger house on Ocean Boulevard and had the famous Beverly Hills decorator, Bernard Gelbort, completely redo it; and they had Gelbort's associate, Robert Crowder, do the exquisite decorative panels. At one time, as many as five hundred workmen were busy getting this huge mansion in shape to suit the Donahues.

New plumbing was put into the twenty-two bathrooms. The walls were covered in hand-woven silks, on top of which might repose a Rosa Bonheur painting or its equivalent. In the drawing room there was an altar that rose to the high ceiling; the altar came from the private chapel of Diane de Montaigne. A curio cabinet held rare jades and porcelain and F.W.'s gold watch, which was kept in pristine condition.

They had a home of equal splendor in Southampton.

After about a year in the new house in Palm Beach, Wooly's condition, which had worsened, resulted in a heart attack. He keeled over in front of the television set. He died as he was born, in regal splendor.

In his will, Wooly left Mary an amount equal to half the value of the adjusted gross estate, after taxes, plus all three houses, including furnishings and contents.

According to previous divorce agreements, trust funds had been set up for his two former wives and his daughter.

To The American Museum of Natural History in New York City, he willed articles of anthropological or scientific interest, including his hunting trophies and mounted wild animal heads, housed at the Calverton lodge.

We doubt that Mary felt hurt at not receiving these. Those silken walls were not woven to hold them.

Chapter 8

Uncle Sam Inherits

Would you believe that since 1862 the U. S. Government has inherited $41,267,943.72? One of the largest bequests came from Justice Oliver Wendell Holmes of the U. S. Supreme Court. Out of an estate of $350,000, a grateful government received $220,372.01, the residue he had willed it after certain other bequests.

Hundreds of immigrants express their gratitude for the good life they've had in this country by willing their sometimes meager, sometimes quite substantial, savings to the United States.

The Treasury Department was so pleased over a bequest of $85,000 from a truck driver named William Meitz that it put out a publicity release on the story in October 1971. The release says: "Teamsters Union President Frank Fitzsimmons formally informed Treasury Secretary George P. Shultz and Labor Secretary James Hodgson that $85,000 had been given to the Government today from the estate of William Meitz, a St. Louis Teamster Union member, who willed his entire estate to the U. S. Government.

"Mr. Meitz, a bachelor, was 81 when he died on January 3, 1972. He had worked as a driver for 37 years with the firm of Beck and Corbitt in St. Louis.

"Mr. Meitz's will read that 'my estate of whatever kind and character and wherever situated, I give and bequeath to the Government of the U.S. to be used by said Government in any manner that it sees fit.'"

Secretary Hodgson remarked that "This is a real example of the industriousness, thrift and success of the modern American working man. Mr. Meitz's bequest is a true symbol of the working man's love of country."

Secretary Shultz noted that Mr. Meitz, a World War I veteran, had accumulated his money by investing in U. S. Savings Bonds, an indication of his many years of devotion to his country. Shultz said, "It is the contributions, both in spirit and savings, of millions of hard-working union men and women and other citizens such as Mr. Meitz that provide the real muscle and strength of the United States."

Not many of the bequests to the government are given the public attention that Mr. Meitz's legacy received, but quite a few of them merit a few lines in the newspapers, an indication that such bequests are rare enough to be newsworthy. A few are quoted here, to indicate the general tenor of the wills leaving such bequests.

A frugal wheat and cattle farmer named Esley H. Sproat, who died in his unheated, unpainted house in Nebraska in 1961, said in his will, "I am grateful to my country for the blessings of freedom it has given to me and for the opportunity to acquire, hold and own property," and thereupon left an estimated $250,000 to the U. S. Government.

Mrs. Anna Krinsk left Russia to seek a new homeland of freedom and found it in the United States. Her husband, also a Russian immigrant, had predeceased her. Written with a pen on a torn page of a tablet, Mrs. Krinsk's will read, "I give all my property to Uncel Sam of Amerika who was help to adopt me. I was so happy to liven in Amerika. I gratitude to only Uncel Sam and He will know what to do with my property." The estate was in excess of $10,000.

The late Miss Annie Bronson of Boston, secretary to a Harvard law professor, saved $100,000 over the years. She had never met Senator Henry Byrd, but admired him greatly and corresponded with him frequently on general legislative matters. Upon her demise she left him her estate to be used "as he saw fit for the benefit of the United States."

Albert Hoffman came to this country from Austria and remained for thirty years until his death. He stated in his will that one of the greatest regrets of his life was that he had not become an American citizen. To make amends, out of an estate of $6,000, he left $4,200 of it to the United States of America in consideration of the many years of happiness he found in its freedom and under its protection.

Jacob Ramar, a retired U. S. Army corporal, died in his sleep in a rooming house in Miami, leaving a note behind that willed $14,900 to the U. S. Government.

Bertrand Larramendy, who died in California in 1969 at the age of eighty-three, said in his last, very brief will, "Because I am extremely grateful to have lived in this country, I leave my entire estate to the government of the United States of America." The amount involved was $171,682. Larramendy emigrated to the United States from France, worked as a general handyman in lumber camps, and kept investing his money in stocks and houses. He himself lived in a $12,000 house in downtown Sacramento. Apparently Larramendy thought more of his adopted country and the financial advantages it offered than he did of his cousins, sisters, and a stepbrother scattered all over the world. They were each allotted one dollar.

The United States is not the only government to benefit from legacies in wills. Dr. John Lewis Horn, a retired college professor, admired the democratic concept of Israel so much that even though he himself was a Gentile, he left an estate valued at more than $860,000 for the benefit of land reclamation in Israel, the Medical Relief Association, and for financing young immigrants who wished to go to Israel.

In London, Paul H. M. Oppenheimer left the bulk of his estate for "the reduction of the national debt." The British Treasury found itself about $450,000 richer, not to mention the $265,000 it collected in inheritance taxes first.

The will of Mrs. George Bernard Shaw, who was Irish-born, indicated that she loved her native land to the extent that she left $263,200 "to polish the manners of the Irish." The will was verbose, one sentence alone containing 150 words, but as far as the court could make out she wanted some sort of finishing school for the Irish people to teach them "self control, elocu-

tion, deportment, the arts of personal contact and social intercourse." An official of the National City Bank of Dublin told
reporters the trustees were gratified but a little confused as
to just how the objects of the will could be realized. One sug-
gestion from a Dublin University professor and a former director of the famous Abbey Theatre was that the money should
be used to endow traveling dramatic companies and acting
schools to give the Irish "the artistic nourishment for which
our people are by and large starved."

The U. S. Treasury gets numerous gifts of cash that are not
in the form of legacies. During a few months in 1972 the mail
brought Treasury headquarters $27,062 from people who asked
that it be used to retire the national debt. During the same
time period, taxpayers who didn't have to, sent the government $3,540.53 that was earmarked for national defense. Many
donors sent $500 to keep the Voice of America on the air. In
addition to contributions earmarked for special federal pro-
grams or problems, the Treasury Department also ends up
with "conscience money" donations from people who believe
they wronged the government at some time. These contributions are almost always anonymous. There is a special procedure for handling "conscience money." Workers who handle
the "conscience mail" section sit in pairs, one opening, one
watching, as the letters come in. The opener and watcher both
sign the slip indicating the amount received, and the money
eventually winds up in the U. S. Treasury. That office got
$46,373.59 during the 1971–72 fiscal year.

Outright gifts to Uncle Sam, above and beyond "conscience
money," totaled $1,123,015.44 during 1972. The biggest years
before that for gifts and legacies were 1943, 1944, and 1945;
the government received $3,892,899.24 in 1943, $2,794,338.91
in 1944, and $2,871,362.28 in 1945. Another banner year was
1968, when $1,318,913.10 reached the Treasury till.

The government's worst year, as far as receiving gifts goes,
was 1892, when it only got ten cents. The year 1864 wasn't
much better, as only fifty cents came in then. In 1875 a dollar
was received, yet only four years later, in 1883, a whopping

$971,360 came in. It is interesting to note that during the war years 1914–18 very small amounts, totaling less than $10,000 came in each year, yet during the war years 1942–45 well over $2 million was received in bequests each year.

Money willed to the government is credited to a special account on the books of the Treasury for "Gifts to the United States," and this account is part of the general revenues of the United States. The money itself goes into the general checking account and loses its identity. The use of the general fund is consistent with the desires of Congress. It is possible, however, to bequeath money to special funds authorized by Congress, such as certain Defense Department activities and the Library of Congress.

Chapter 9
The Will of a Sex Symbol

In life beautiful Marilyn Monroe ran the gamut of human emotions and experiences, including the misery of being unloved, fear of insanity, the joy of being loved, insecurity, occasional security, addiction to pills and liquor, fame, censure, a plethora of sex, and intimacy with celebrities in all fields, including the President of the United States. It was all too much for a sickly, fearful girl, and she tried to end her life on innumerable occasions. The last attempt succeeded, if that particular time was an attempt. Or was it just another occasion when she mixed alcohol and sleeping pills?

Marilyn died with the telephone in her hand. There has been much speculation as to whom she was calling, or trying to call. Her last known telephone conversation was with actor Peter Lawford, who had introduced her to his brothers-in-law, President John Kennedy and Bobby Kennedy, and with both of whom she was rumored to have been on cozy terms. Lawford had called to see why she was late in coming to his house for dinner. Marilyn replied in a slurred voice that she was too tired to come to dinner. Then surprisingly she said, "Say goodbye to Pat [Lawford's wife], say goodbye to the President, and say goodbye to yourself because you're a nice guy."

Through Lawford's efforts the psychiatric nurse staying with Marilyn was contacted. She went to the closed door of Marilyn's room, saw the light on and heard the record player going, and assumed Marilyn was all right. The nurse got up at 3:30 A.M., saw the light still on under Marilyn's locked door, went out and peered through the bedroom window, and saw Marilyn with the phone in her hand, lying motionless on the bed.

A doctor was called and pronounced her dead. Thus ended a life that had become too unhappy to endure.

From the very beginning, life had been tough, and those miserable early days undoubtedly set the pattern for what was to follow. Her birth certificate read: "Girl, born June 1, 1926, to Gladys Baker. Father unknown." She was named Norma Jean Baker. Gladys's other two children by a previous marriage, Jack and Berneice, lived with their father. Gladys was working, and boarded Norma Jean with a family she knew, but finally scraped up enough money to make a down payment on a house and took in boarders so she could look after the child. When Norma Jean was nine her mother Gladys became violently insane, as had *her* mother Della, her grandfather, and her uncle, previously. Norma Jean was placed in the Los Angeles Orphanage for two years, then removed to a temporary home where, she later recounted, she was first "used" by men. Perversely, this was the first time she had felt loved and wanted.

At sixteen Norma Jean married a handsome boy named Jim Dougherty, and when he was called into service she took a job at a plane company, where she was "discovered" by a Conover photographer. Her face appeared on magazine covers. Tom Kelly immortalized her with that famous nude photograph of her used on a calendar, which sold in the millions. Things moved fast after that. She was taken under the wing of sixty-nine-year-old producer Joe Schenck, who introduced her to actor-casting director Ben Lyon. Lyon advised some minor plastic surgery and had her change her name to Marilyn Monroe. During her meteoric rise as a movie star, Marilyn dusted off her young husband and had affairs with countless men. Her relationships with her employers were strained because of Marilyn's unpunctuality and lack of confidence, which led her to insomnia and the use of barbiturates.

All the details of Marilyn's marriages to Joe DiMaggio and playwright Arthur Miller have been faithfully recorded by numerous biographers. But few of those biographers get around to mentioning the power behind the throne in Marilyn's life—

a tiny but charming agent named Johnny Hyde. He became her agent when she was just starting out as a starlet, he loved her, and she remained loyal to him until the day he died. She loved him, too, in a very special way. He took her to all the "in" places where she would be seen, and to tell the truth, she wasn't particularly noticeable in the early days. She was just another pretty girl with brown hair. The big difference came when she became a blonde and started wearing the right kind of clothes to show off her spectacular figure. When she became famous, other, bigger, more important agents tried to lure her into their camp, but she remained with little Johnny until he died of a heart attack.

Marilyn was eternally grateful to those who showed her special kindness and consideration, and proved it in her will. Her gross estate came to $90,000, plus 10 percent distributors' gross of *Some Like It Hot* and her last picture, *Misfits*. The will left a bequest of $5,000 to Norman and Hedda Rosten, who had befriended her while she was with Arthur Miller. If they predeceased her, the bequest went to their daughter Patricia, to be used for her education. To May Reis, whom Marilyn had hired to handle her correspondence and who became her best friend, she left the sum of $40,000, or 25 percent of the remainder of the estate, whichever should be the less. Her half sister Berneice Miracle was bequeathed $10,000. Lee Strasberg, director of the Actors' Studio, and his wife Paula showed great friendship for and had a profound influence on Marilyn, and she remembered that in making out her will. Strasberg received all of Marilyn's personal effects and clothing, to be distributed by him "among my friends, colleagues and those to whom I am devoted." He also inherited the residue of the estate. Marilyn's mother Gladys Baker was to receive $5,000 per annum in quarterly payments for the remainder of her life.

One of Marilyn's coaches was Michael Chekhov, and when he died she continued sending gifts to his wife. In her will Marilyn left Mrs. Chekhov $2,500 per annum, in quarterly payments, during her lifetime.

Upon the death of either Gladys Baker or Mrs. Michael Chekhov, the trust allotted to them was to be turned over to Dr. Marianne Kris (one of Marilyn's doctors), to be used by her for the furtherance of the work of psychiatric institutions or groups.

Inez Nelson, conservator of Gladys Baker, instructed an attorney to object to the will, claiming that Marilyn was under the influence of Lee Strasberg or Marianne Kris, or both, and to ask for more money for Mrs. Baker. That claim was denied.

Due to tax problems involving legal residency and future taxes to be paid on residuals continuing to come in from reruns in movies and on television of *Some Like It Hot* and *The Misfits*, the estate has not yet been settled. It remains as mixed up as Marilyn was in life.

Toward the end Marilyn was constantly talking to her lawyer Milton Rudin about changing her will. Rudin managed to avoid the subject. There was a question in the minds of all her friends by then as to whether Marilyn was of sound mind.

Naturally the sex life of the leading sex symbol was, and still is, the leading topic when Marilyn is discussed. Of particular interest is the question of whether she had affairs with Bobby or Jack Kennedy. According to Earl Wilson, Marilyn herself helped start the gossip. She told a friend that while visiting in New York she slipped out for a meeting with President Kennedy and "made his back feel better." (Of course, it's possible she just took along some Baume Bengué.) She was frequently seen boarding one of the Kennedy planes. She met Bobby Kennedy in the Lawford home on occasion. Because of her reputation, it was assumed that practically every encounter Marilyn had led straight to the bedroom.

If their names had been Jack and Bobby Zilch, rather than Jack and Bobby Kennedy, those meetings between them and Marilyn would only have caused a shrug of the shoulders. But since they *were* the President and Attorney General of the United States, the speculation as to whether Marilyn had affairs with either or both still runs high. There have even been far-fetched suggestions that Marilyn was "rubbed out" for fear she would reveal state secrets whispered to her between the sheets. It seems safe to assume that political matters would be the very last subject discussed under such conditions.

There is no question that sex was a way of life for Marilyn—something as taken for granted as, say, bathing or shaking hands. It made her feel loved and wanted from the age of eleven on. It was a means of gaining friends and objectives, and of momentarily feeling important.

She thought nothing of it when, at one of his parties, Joe Schenck suggested to a newspaperman present—in front of Marilyn—that the newsman take her upstairs and f—— her. Nor was Marilyn shy about discussing her affairs. Once when her dramatic coach commented that her face was all red, Marilyn replied "Howard [Hughes] hasn't shaved in four days."

It has been hinted by some of those who have had affairs with her that in reality Marilyn didn't care all that much about sex—that it was just something to be done and gotten over with. In other words, she wasn't really a nymphomaniac. Certainly sex and love were two entirely different words to her. Sex was for almost anybody. Love was for a very chosen few. Love was for two of her husbands, Joe DiMaggio and Arthur Miller, and for Yves Montand, one of her leading men, who didn't marry her because he already had a wife. Sex meant keeping up the image of a sex symbol. Love was what this insecure woman yearned for.

Marilyn found an enduring love in Joe DiMaggio. They always remained close, even after their divorce. Joe is the one who claimed her body when she died, and arranged the funeral. Joe is the one who still sends roses to her burial place every single week since she died. Joe actually resented her image as a sex symbol, and watched with rage during the filming of a scene for *The Seven-Year Itch* when Marilyn stood over a grating with air blowing her skirts waist high and photographers aimed their lenses up her legs.

Actually, wearing panties for Marilyn was a concession. Ordinarily she wore nothing under her dresses.

Chapter 10

Two Famous Drunks

W. C. Fields and John Barrymore couldn't possibly have been less alike. Fields was the son of a vegetable and fruit hawker. Barrymore sprang from the aristocracy of the theatrical world, with four generations of thespians behind him. Fields was homely. Barrymore was one of the handsomest matinee idols who ever lived. Fields was a comedian. Barrymore was a dramatic actor. The one thing they had in common was that they both ended up drunks. The difference was that people laughed *with* Fields, as a drunk, while they laughed *at* Barrymore when he made a fool of himself acting in a play while drunk. Many women crossed both their paths, and both had tangled marital lives. The difference in the end was that Fields ended up rich, leaving an estate in excess of $700,000 (which didn't include many of the bank accounts he had under fictitious names, which were never discovered), and Barrymore ended up poor, with his estate in bankruptcy.

Having been so poor in his youth, Fields had a phobia about ever being without funds again, plus a tendency toward secretiveness. He opened up bank accounts wherever he went, often under assumed names, and boasted one time that he had over seven hundred accounts all over the world.

His great love when he died was Carlotta Monti, but after his death his estranged wife Harriet and son Claude took over. Fields had specified that his body be placed in an inexpensive coffin and cremated, with no funeral of any kind. Harriet was a Catholic, and would not allow the cremation. A simple nonsectarian service was first performed, with Edgar Bergen officiating. A second, Catholic service followed. Then Carlotta had a third service at the sealed crypt, a spiritualistic reading. In the squabbling over his money, Fields was largely forgotten. For two years he lay in an anonymous crypt at the luxurious Forest Lawn Cemetery, a place he had frequently derided. The will was fought in the courts for four years.

Fields' will bequeathed his wife "Hattie" and son Claude the sum of $20,000, to be divided equally. Carlotta Monti was to receive $25 a week until $25,000 had been paid. Carlotta was also bequeathed Fields' Cadillac, two bottles of Shalimar perfume, his dictionary, encyclopedia, recording equipment, and various household items. To his brother Walter, Fields left $5,000, to be paid in installments, plus $75 a week for life. His sister Adel was given $5,000, plus $60 a week for life. His brother LeRoy and sister Elsie May each received $500. Fields then named nine friends in the will, with sums ranging from $500 to $5,000, plus household gifts so numerous it would be a complete inventory of the house, grounds, cabinets, files, and drawers. Even two fly catchers were included in the bequests.

Under California community property laws, Fields' estranged wife Harriet claimed half the estate. She also claimed that he had given gifts totaling $482,450 without her consent to various persons, and under the same property laws claimed half of that. On the latter she settled for $65,000.

There was a strange clause in Fields' will, considering the fact that he loathed children, especially working with them. The will stipulated that upon the death of Walter, Adel, and Carlotta, his executors form a corporation under the name of "W. C. Fields College for orphan white boys and girls, where no religion of any sort is to be preached. Harmony is the purpose of this thought." Between the court squabbles and the lawyers' fees over the years, nothing ever came of the orphanage.

Barrymore's will, written a year before he died, declared that he was unmarried, having been divorced from four previous wives, and he expressly made no provisions for them. He stipulated that his executors employ doctors and pay any bills incurred by them for the purpose of ascertaining that he was in fact dead and not in any other state having the semblance of death, in order as far as possible to avoid all risks of being buried alive.

All of his estate, real and personal, was to be divided equally among his three children, Diana, Dolores, and John, Jr. To his daughter Dolores, Barrymore expressly willed "that certain family letter from Abraham Lincoln to Mrs. Louisa Drew dated June 25, 1864, and that certain painting or crayon of me by Sargent." To his son John, Jr., he willed "that certain marble head and bust of me." His gardener, Mark Nishimura, was willed Barrymore's dog. Due to large tax arrears, the estate was placed in bankruptcy.

The marble bust willed to his son John, done by the famous sculptor Paul Manship, was sold to Lionel Barrymore, brother of the deceased. When Lionel died, John sued to obtain the bust. The court approved the sale of it to him for $200.

Chapter 11

A Dreamer's Will

When it came to writing his will, the imagination and fantasy that enabled Robert Ruark to write eleven books and a syndicated column, and to vary the facts of his own life with each telling, were still in full swing. He left most generous bequests to friends and employees, but unfortunately the wherewithal was not there with which to honor them. His publisher had to bring out two posthumous books, called *Use Enough Gun* and *Women,* in order to be paid off for what Ruark died owing them. Hopefully in this case "it's the thought that counts." He certainly meant well, and perhaps when the estate is all settled it might end well too.

Ruark was always given to braggadocio and hyperbole as regards his literary standing and monetary worth. He once turned against an old friend who made the mistake of pausing a moment to think it over when Ruark asked her, "When Hemingway, O'Hara, and Steinbeck are gone, who do you think is going to replace all of them?" The obvious answer apparently was, "Why you, of course, Mr. Ruark."

Whatever his faults were, Ruark had a colorful, lusty, exciting, and often frustrating life, and was extremely talented. The pen-and-ink sketches he drew himself to illustrate *Horn of the Hunter* proved his talent as an artist as well as a writer. His one great frustration in life was the fact that he was never able to surpass or even equal the success of his idol, Ernest Hemingway. But from the beginning of his literary career he tried to emulate Hemingway. Hemingway had written a great deal about Cuba, where he lived, so Ruark went to Cuba and wrote about it in a book called *Grenadine Etching*. Hemingway wrote about Africa, so Ruark went to Africa, got his own white hunter named Harry Selby, and collected not only every animal possible but also the lore that enabled him to turn out *Horn of the Hunter, Something of Value,* and *Uhuru.*

Eventually Ruark turned against killing animals and gave up on Africa, but not on the animal heads and rugs that covered every room of his home in Spain. He might have been influenced on giving up Africa by the fact that he was no longer welcome there after *Uhuru* came out.

It wasn't just Hemingway's writing that Ruark tried to emulate, or the hunting. He also manfully tried to follow the master's example in boozing, wenching, boasting, and fighting, and enjoyed quite a success in all fields. It was the boozing that finally did him in.

Ruark started out as a sportswriter in Washington, D.C., graduated to a syndicated general column for Scripps-Howard in New York, and eventually moved to the Costa Brava in Spain to avoid paying the high income taxes he had always resented.

His books always portrayed Ruark's thoughts and attitudes. *Poor No More* reflected some of the bitterness of his child-hood. Ruark often talked about the unhappiness of his early life. Whether true or not, he often said that his parents were nutty and he had to have them in numerous institutions. The grandfather of his books and articles on *The Old Man and the Boy* was, he admitted, a figment of his fertile imagination. Hemingway had an old man in *The Old Man and the Sea*—so Ruark needed an old man too.

The Honey Badger, written after his divorce from his wife of twenty-five years, Virginia, summed up his bitter thoughts on marriage and life in general. The book was so named "because the honey badger attacks a man at his groin." The book absolutely devastated Virginia and her parents, who were easily discernible characters in it.

At the time he died, Ruark was engaged to Marilyn Kaytor, cooking editor of *Look* magazine. His ex-wife Virginia died a year after Ruark, of cancer and a broken heart. Because of her illness, Ruark had thought Virginia would predecease him. The fact that she didn't was what held up the settlement of his will.

Here's the bequest that caused all the legal hassles: "I give, devise and bequeath to my friend Marilyn Kaytor, if she survives me, all real property in Palamos [Spain] owned by me and described in a deed conveying title dated January 30, 1963, entered into between Mrs. Virginia W. Ruark and myself." In Ruark's divorce settlement with Virginia she was given half of the house, but sold out her half to Ruark for $100,000, with a proviso that if the house was sold for more than $200,000 she was to receive half of the excess amount. When Virginia died she left her estate to her niece and nephew. Their attorneys started proceedings to force the sale. The courts decreed that the divorce settlement had precedence over the will, and that caused the subsequent court wrangling. Kaytor and Virginia's heirs finally settled out of court for half the profits each when the property is sold.

In the meantime, all the other legatees are sitting it out. Ruark generously willed fifty thousand dollars to his secretary, Alan Ritchie; twenty-five thousand dollars to Deborah Ruby (an employment agency executive in New York and close pal of Ruark's); twenty-five thousand dollars to Eva M. Monley (an assistant movie director who was born in Kenya and became Ruark's close friend); ten thousand dollars to Christina Viu Salamero, his housekeeper; ten thousand dollars to Pascual Munoz Romero, his gardener; and five thousand dollars to Carmen Viu Casagran, another employee at the house. Of course, none of these bequests has been paid off. However, the household help are still occupying the house in Palamos.

Ruark's literary mentor, Harold Matson, was bequeathed Ruark's Rolls-Royce, but it is still sitting in Spain covered with tarpaulin. That Rolls-Royce was Raurk's greatest pride and joy, as for a long time he and Generalissimo Franco were the only two Rolls-Royce owners in Spain. During the sad little funeral parade from Ruark's home in Palamos to the village cemetery, the mourners all walked behind the empty Rolls-

Royce, like the riderless horse of a dead leader. One could almost hear Ruark saying, "What a way to go!"

His house on the beach near Palamos was Ruark's first real home of his own, and was uppermost in his mind when writing his will. For instance, he stipulated that Eva M. Monley, Deborah Ruby, Sonia Ritchie, York Kilday, Harold Matson, Alan McIntyre Ritchie, and Paul Gitlin could, without rental or other cost, have equal but separate and independent use and occupancy of the property during their lifetimes, from time to time and for such periods as the trustees deemed appropriate to effect such purpose. That clause could really have caused some haggling as to which of the seven persons named could have the house, and when Ruark further stipulated that upon the death of the last survivor of those seven named, the trustees should pay over and transfer the property to the University of North Carolina, at Chapel Hill, absolutely and forever, "it being my desire that the University of North Carolina retain the property for educational purposes, possibly as an 'off-campus' facility, for sabbaticals for faculty, and in general to take advantage of the geographical and physical setting of said property."

Of course, none of those stipulations can be carried out, as the house must be sold as a result of the court case between Marilyn Kaytor and Virginia Ruark's heirs.

Strangely enough, the will of Bob Ruark's idol, Ernest Hemingway, mainly concerned his farm, called Finca Vigia, in San Francisco de Paula, Cuba. Off and on, Hemingway had spent twenty-five of his best and most productive years on that Cuban farm, and that is where he wrote his will on September 17, 1955—six years before he put a gun in his mouth and pulled the trigger, on his western ranch. The will was quite simple. It gave all his property to his wife Mary, whom he appointed his executrix, and stipulated that she was to provide for his children. Mary gave the Finca Vigia to Castro, who has made the house into a museum of sorts, which can be visited by appointment only. Castro has observed his promise to Mary Hemingway not to propagandize the place as the shrine of a renowned American who applauded his revolution. However, it *is* maintained as a shrine to him—the very thing Ruark would have loved to happen to *his* house in Spain.

Castro invited a couple of dozen American reporters to Havana and Santiago de Cuba in 1964 to take a well-programmed look at how he was making out. One of those reporters, Bob Considine, visited Hemingway's place, twelve miles out of Havana. Here is his report on that visit:

The house is as he left it on July 24, 1960, to go to Pamplona to see the bulls run and to explain "Bloody Summer," his disappointing account of the mano-a-manos tour of Antonio Ordonez and Luis Dominguin.

There are fresh flowers everywhere in the house, and the airy place is spotless. His favorite chair is still there in what must be called the living room. It is done in a chintzy pink print that is at odds with the heads of menacing beasts glaring down from the walls. The bar table still nudges at an arm of the deep chair, offering a variety of lived-with half-empties. A large metal ice bucket snuggles at the foot of the bar. I had an uneasy feeling that it might be filled. There is a footstool near the chair on which Hemingway left a number of items he was reading or planned to read. On top of the pile is Allan Villers' "Give Me a Ship to Sail." Luncheon for three is always about to be served at Finca la Vigia, but never is. The table is set each noon by Rene Villaralo, a now middle-aged Cuban brought into the menage as a child to be a companion to Hemingway's sons. The china, silver, and glassware glitter from careful attention. The table flowers are sparkling fresh. There will be two wines. Papa will sit in the big chair facing Miss Mary and the guest beside her. . . .

It was something of a relief to get the hell out of the dining room.

Villaralo led us into Hemingway's combination bedroom-work-room. Directing our attention to the freshly made double bed on which there were a number of books and magazines and a Helen Wills white sun visor, he said that the master often fell asleep late at night amid such debris. This was what he had rolled in during his last night in that bed, the good and faithful servant said with his emotions gathering like a storm.

Ruark's "Poor No More" lay near one of the pillows of the uncommonly short bed. How much that would have meant to Bob!

Hemingway wrote standing up, his man recalled. He showed us the plain white bookcase that rose about as high as the author's once-barreled chest. He used its top layer as a desk. Hemingway would confront it every morning, write down his thoughts in longhand with a pencil, and then transcribe them on a beat-up portable he had carried through at least one war. That was atop another bookcase, where he also breakfasted: juice, tea, Ry-Krisp. He always wrote in his bare feet, Villaralo told us, because he could not think with his shoes on. In the wintertime he would protect his feet from the cold tiles with a thin rug made from the skin of some small animal he had shot. He kept a bookkeeper's account of how many words he wrote each day and marked the total on a writing board which would not be out of place in a drugstore inventory. Sometimes he wrote as many as seventeen hundred words a day ("if he was going fishing the next day," Villaralo explained). Sometimes he wrote only three hundred. Sometimes he just stared. He never used his regular desk except as a kind of display table. The day I was there it held a collection of bullets of different caliber, lined up like

smart troops, his war correspondent brassard, a snap-
shot of Mary, and one of Marlene Dietrich singing to
gaping GI's. Under the glass top of the desk was an
illuminated religious card, a prayer of Ignatius
Loyola: "Soul of Christ, sanctify me. . . . Soul of
Christ, save me."

Chapter 12

The Unlucky Hope Diamond

Mrs. Evalyn Walsh McLean was mainly known for her possession of the world-famous Hope diamond, one of the best-known and most historically exciting jewels in the world. Closer to home, in Washington, D.C., where she was chatelaine of a large estate called "Friendship," she was known for her humanity, her humility, her efforts on behalf of servicemen during the war, her numerous parties, and her courage in the face of one tragedy after another.

Were those tragedies caused by her unlucky Hope diamond? The diamond had a long history of bringing bad luck to its owners. Yet Mrs. McLean loved to wear it so much it became her trademark. She had her portrait painted wearing it, and kept her home guarded so she could keep the diamond with her rather than keeping it in a vault. She wore it with both daytime and evening clothing, hanging from a diamond-and-platinum chain around her neck, and loved to show it off to interested friends or even strangers.

The diamond was offered for sale to Mrs. McLean in Paris by Pierre Cartier, and several months later, in January of 1911, she purchased it in Washington. She was fascinated not only by the rare, deep sapphire blue and flawless purity of the 44½-carat diamond, but also by its exciting history. Stolen from the forehead of a Hindu idol and smuggled out of India by a French adventurer named Jean Tavernier, the rough diamond, then weighing 112½ carats, was sold to Louis XIV. The King liked the diamond for himself, but when his mistress desired and got it, she fell out of favor. The story on Tavernier's fate varies. In one version he was torn to death by dogs. In another he was rewarded with a fortune and a title, but the fortune was dissipated by his dissolute son, and at over 80 years of age he was obliged to return to India, where he died in a vain attempt to recoup.

Meanwhile, the 112½-carat rough was ordered recut by Louis XIV into a 67½-carat pear shape, and this became part of the French Crown Jewels and was known as the "French Blue." Some 125 years later, when the French Revolution burst forth, this stone, together with the royal jewels and regalia, were confiscated by the revolutionary authorities. The gems were carefully placed for safekeeping in the French Treasury, but in September 1792 the entire treasure was stolen. The guillotining of Louis XVI and Marie Antoinette was thought to be part of the curse of owning the diamond.

A great part of the royal treasure was recovered through an anonymous tip, but the "French Blue" was not among the jewels returned to the French Treasury. The gem didn't turn up until 1830 when, in its present oval shape, weighing 44½ carats, the diamond mysteriously reappeared in London in the hands of a certain Daniel Eliason. Though recut to disguise its origin, the dark sapphire blue color of the gem left no doubt that it was part of the missing "French Blue." It was purchased by an English banker named Henry Thomas Hope for a reputed 90,000 pounds, and became known as the Hope diamond. Hope gave the stone to his daughter, the Duchess of Newcastle, who left it to her son, Lord Francis Pelham Clinton. Clinton gave it to his bride, May Yohe, a music hall entertainer. Then the curse started working again. May eloped, leaving the diamond behind, and ended up as a scrubwoman.

In about 1900 the diamond was purchased by agents for the Sultan Abdul Hamid of Turkey for $400,000. That is when Evalyn Walsh McLean came into the picture. One of the few women of the Western world ever to visit the inner sanctum of the Turkish Court, she saw the great gem gleaming from the Sultan's turban, and dreamed of possessing it one day. Shortly before the Young Turks' Revolt the Sultan, anticipating a hasty withdrawal, sent several of his agents to Paris for the purpose of disposing of the Hope diamond and several other great gems. That's when Cartier offered it to Mrs. McLean.

Evalyn Walsh McLean's own bad luck, after acquiring the Hope diamond, started with her husband Edward B. McLean, son of the multimillionaire publisher of the Cincinnati *Enquirer* and the Washington *Post*. Edward Beale McLean, called "Ned," carried on a long romance with Rose Davies, sister of Marion Davies, and made many attempts to divorce Evalyn so he could marry Rose. He even went so far as to obtain a divorce in Latvia, but it was never recognized in the United States. Six months later, at Mrs. McLean's petition, McLean was declared by a sheriff's jury at Towson, Maryland, to be insane and incapable of managing his affairs. He was kept at the Shepard and Enoch Pratt Hospital, near Baltimore, where he died at the age of fifty-eight.

McLean's will, dated June 9, 1931, bequeathed $300,000 to Rose Davies and cut off his wife with only her dower rights. It cut off his three children, Jock, Ned, Jr., and Evalyn with $5,000 each, but awarded $100,000 each to Martin Finn, his former valet, and John Major, his ex-bodyguard. The will had no meaning, however, as the family attorneys stepped in with the bad news that Ned McLean had died broke. His father had left him an income for life only, and the McLean estate automatically reverted to the family, will or no will.

Even before the trouble with her husband, tragedy had struck Evalyn. Her first child was killed in a traffic accident. The worst blow of all came just a few months before Mrs. McLean died of pneumonia in 1947. Her only daughter, Evalyn Reynolds, wife of ex-Senator Robert Rice Reynolds of North Carolina, died from an apparent overdose of sleeping pills at the age of 25. Mrs. McLean never recovered from that tragedy and remained in virtual seclusion until her own death a few months later.

There is a widespread legend that Mrs. McLean would never allow any of her children to touch the diamond, for fear it would bring them bad luck. Son Jock denies that story, however, saying he was "teethed on the Hope diamond."

Until Evalyn acquired that unlucky stone, she had known only good luck. She was born in a two-room log cabin, the daughter of a miner named John R. Walsh. One night her father woke her up and said, "Father struck it rich." (She later wrote a book of that title.) From then on Evalyn was reared like a princess, and the Walsh trust accounted for a good part of the inheritance she left.

In her will Mrs. McLean requested that her trustees, Bishop Fulton J. Sheen, Father Edmund A. Walsh (vice president of Georgetown University), Thurman Arnold (former Assistant Attorney General), and Associate Justice Frank Murphy of the U. S. Supreme Court, put her jewelry away in safekeeping until after all the following of her grandchildren reached the age of 25 years: John R. McLean, Evalyn Walsh McLean, Mamie Spears Reynolds, Emily McLean, and Edward B. McLean II. At that time her jewelry should be distributed with the rest of her property to these and any future grandchildren. At the time the estate was appraised, the Hope diamond was valued at $176,920. Another diamond, the Star of the East, received the valuation of $185,-000. Her renowned jewels also included a pigeon-blood ruby, said to be the largest of its kind in the country.

Two years after Mrs. McLean's death, Thurman Arnold, the executor, trustees Bishop Sheen and Father Walsh, and her two sons, Jock and Ned (Frank Murphy having renounced his appointment both as executor and trustee under the will), petitioned for authority to sell the jewelry to provide funds for the payment of debts and claims against the estate and for the best interest of the trust estate and the beneficiaries. The petition was granted, and the jewelry, which had been appraised at $587,677, was sold privately to Harry Winston, a Fifth Avenue jeweler, for $611,500. It was agreed that it would have been too difficult to divide the jewelry evenly among the grandchildren anyhow.

Not long after purchasing the jewelry Harry Winston, anx-

ious that the Smithsonian Institution should have a jewel
room, gave the Hope diamond to the Institution, where it is
now a stellar attraction. He sold the rest of the jewelry to
private buyers.

Except for her family, Mrs. McLean's other bequests were
few. She gave her butler and her watchman each $500, and
directed that three other employees receive a monthly re-
mittance as long as they lived. She gave her son-in-law, Robert
Rice Reynolds, the husband of her beloved deceased daughter, the use of "Friendship," her Washington house, during
his lifetime, saying "he showed such love and consideration
for my daughter that he richly deserves to be fully considered
in this matter." All her other real and personal property, except her jewelry, was to be held in trust for her two sons,
John R. and Edward McLean.

Another stipulation said: "Because my granddaughter
Mamie Spears Reynolds is living with me and because of my
special interest and concern for her, I direct that, regardless
of any previous provisions of this will, my trustees shall use
any and all funds to assure that Mamie Spears Reynolds is
adequately provided for until she shall have reached the age
of 25 years. If necessary to carry out the purposes of this provision, I direct that the bequest to Robert Rice Reynolds
and to my sons John R. and Edward McLean may be diverted to this purpose and that my jewelry may be taken
out of safekeeping and sold for this purpose."

Apparently Mrs. McLean wasn't too sure her creditors
would not try to take advantage of her after her death, as
she also made this stipulation: "I direct my executors to pay
all of my just debts as soon as practicable after my decease,
but inasmuch as I believe that many charges made to me and
bills rendered to me are greater in amount than the sums
actually due from some of my creditors, I direct my executors to investigate the merits of all claims filed and bills presented against my estate, and to contest the payment of any
such bills or claims which in their opinion are excessive and
do not constitute debts for which I am legally liable."

The will was written shortly after the death of her daughter, Evalyn, and five months before Mrs. McLean's own death.

Two more grandchildren came along afterward, Michael Hatrick and Ronald Walsh McLean, the sons of Ned's marriage to the former Gloria Hatrick (who is now married to actor Jimmy Stewart). And bad luck continued to hound the family. Jock's daughter Evalyn died under mysterious circumstances at the age of 25, and Ned's son Ronald, a first lieutenant in the Marines, was killed in Vietnam in 1969.

One wonders what bad luck could possibly befall the Smithsonian Institution, the present owner of the Hope diamond. Or has the curse finally run its course?

Mrs. Jock ("Brownie") McLean insists that all the bad things that have happened concerning Washington, the assassination of President Kennedy and of his brother Robert, the war in Vietnam, the Watergate scandal, etc., have happened since the Smithsonian, a government institution, acquired the diamond. She says even the portrait of Mrs. Evalyn Walsh McLean wearing the diamond brought bad luck. When the Jock McLeans took an apartment in New York City, Jock had the portrait brought up and hung while his wife was out of town. When Brownie got home and saw the portrait, she insisted it be taken away and put in storage. She was afraid of it. While the portrait was standing in a back hall waiting to be picked up by the warehouse, there was a fire in the hall that destroyed everything there but the portrait. When the warehouse truck picked up the portrait, the truck was involved in an accident en route to the warehouse, and the driver broke his leg. The portrait was unharmed. Shortly after that, the driver's wife died unexpectedly. Not long after the portrait was stored in the warehouse, the warehouse burned down—and only the cell containing the portrait remained untouched by the fire. Coincidence? Perhaps. But how does one account for all those other fateful coincidences that happened to people involved with the Hope diamond?

Chapter 13

A Museum Benefits from a Dog Lover

Although Frank Andrew Munsey died nearly half a century ago, he is still remembered—and hated—by old newsmen, because he put so many newspapers and newspapermen out of business. But he still elicits a chuckle from those few people who are "in" on the large bequest he left the Metropolitan Museum of Art.

Munsey started out pleasantly enough as publisher of *Golden Argosy,* a juvenile magazine for which he wrote serials himself. He later changed the magazine to *Argosy,* for adults, and supplanted this with *Munsey's Magazine,* the first ten-cent periodical. When a magazine failed he scrapped it and started another. Thus he disposed of *Godey's Magazine, All-Story Magazine,* and others.

Having failed at publishing magazines, Munsey turned to newspapers. In 1891 he purchased the New York *Star,* changing its name to the *Daily Continent* and making it a pioneer attempt to give the news in tabloid form. It failed. Then, using the fortune he made from a chain of grocery stores and the financial operations of his trust company, he bought several newspapers, hoping to found a chain of them. His purchases included the Baltimore *News,* New York *Press,* New York *Sun,* Boston *Journal,* New York *Daily News,* Washington *Times,* and New York *Herald.* In 1916 Munsey started consolidating papers, and gained the title "executioner of newspapers." He merged the New York *Press* in the *Sun,* and in 1920 the unsuccessful *Sun* in the New York *Herald.* In 1924 he sold the *Herald* to the New York *Tribune,* having meanwhile renamed the *Evening Sun* the *Sun,* and absorbed in it the *Globe* and *Commercial Advertiser.* His last purchase was that of the

New York *Mail,* which he merged in his *Evening Telegram* in 1924. Munsey died in 1925.

His will specified that Munsey was to be buried in the family plot in Lisbon Falls, Maine, and he bequeathed the cemetery $25,000, to be invested, with the income therefrom mainly used to maintain and preserve the Munsey family plot.

Munsey bequeathed stock in the Munsey Trust Company of Washington, D.C., to his sister, Emma J. Hyde, and also to her son and daughter. After generous bequests to twenty-three friends and relatives, Munsey willed $250,000 to Bowdoin College of Brunswick, Maine, $100,000 to the Maine State Hospital of Portland, Maine, and $50,000 to the Central Maine General Hospital of Lewiston, Maine.

All the residue of the estate was willed to the Metropolitan Museum of Art. There is an amusing and oft-repeated legend about that last bequest. It seems that Mr. Munsey was a bit unclear as to what institution was to receive the bulk of his estate. His lawyer is supposed to have said, "How about leaving it to a museum?"

"What museum did you have in mind?" Munsey asked.

"Well, er, ah, how about the Museum of Natural History?"

"What's there? I've never been there."

"Oh, they have stuffed animals in their native habitat, and things like that."

For the first time, Munsey evinced a little interest. "Do they have any stuffed dogs there?"

"Oh yes, they must certainly have some stuffed dogs there."

"Then maybe I should leave it to them. The only thing I ever really loved was my little dog Patsy, that I had from the time I was six until I was seventeen years old. I loved that dog."

"Then of course you might consider the Metropolitan Museum of Art," ventured the lawyer.

"Any dogs there?" asked Munsey.

"Oh yes, they have lots of pictures of dogs there. I particularly remember a painting with two small dogs in it—a charming picture."

"Patsy was a small dog—maybe I should leave it to *them*."

Munsey couldn't seem to make up his mind which of the museums should benefit, according to the legend. A few days later his lawyer put two wills on Munsey's desk with all the specifications the same except that one will left the residue of the estate to the Museum of Natural History and the other left it to the Metropolitan Museum of Art. Busy and still undecided, Munsey reached for the nearer one and signed it. And that is how the Metropolitan Museum of Art was $17,000,-000 richer when the will was probated.

Chapter 14
The Will That Corrupted a Town

When Lebanese poet, painter, and mystic Kahlil Gibran died in 1931 and willed the royalties from seven of his books to the small town of his birth, Bsherri, in the spectacular mountains of Lebanon, he had no idea that the legacy would result in corruption, violence, and murder. He had only kindness and remembrance of things past in his heart when he made the will.

Gibran spent only the first eleven years of his life, from 1883 to 1894, in Bsherri, and they were not terribly happy years. He didn't like to mingle with other children, and was tutored at home, where he learned to speak Arabic, French, and English. His father was an alcoholic, and his mother finally broke away from the father, taking the children to Boston. Kahlil had two sisters, Marianna and Sultana, and a brother, Peter. He returned to Beirut in 1896 to attend school. Concluding his courses with high honors, Kahlil went to Paris in 1901 to study painting for two years, during which he also wrote profusely in Arabic. He wrote *Spirits Rebellious*, which was burned in the marketplace in Beirut soon after its publication. For writing this book Gibran was exiled from his country and excommunicated from the Maronite Catholic Church, the book having been pronounced by it as "dangerous, revolutionary, and poisonous to youth."

Within a year and a half of his return to America, Kahlil's sister Sultana, his brother Peter, and his mother had all died. During this period Gibran gave an exhibition of his paintings, which was attended by Miss Mary Haskell, owner of a school for girls in Boston. From that day until his death, Miss Haskell was his patron and his devotee. Most important, she sent him a monthly allowance of $75, which allowed him to return in 1908 to Paris to study at the Académie Julien and the Beaux Arts. It was here he learned that the new government in Turkey had pardoned all exiles. In 1910 Gibran returned to America, moved to 51 West Tenth Street in New York, and lived there until his death in 1931.

During all these years Gibran was writing as well as painting. He had written and rewritten his most famous book, *The Prophet*, in Arabic several times, as well as several other books in Arabic. As he wrote and painted, he became the nucleus of a salon, with Gibran as high guru, surrounded by adoring women, though he was celibate. Another of his disciples was Barbara Young, who later wrote a book about him that was such a paean of adulation the reader felt he was surreptitiously reading her diary, and was embarrassed. Mary Haskell also wrote a panting book about him. It seems none of his biographers could write otherwise about him.

In 1916 Alfred Knopf, only twenty-three and a newcomer in the book publishing business, was introduced to Gibran, and started frequenting the salon on West Tenth Street. He needed authors, and during the next four years published three of Gibran's books, none of which sold well. In 1923 he brought out *The Prophet*, which had finally been written in English by Gibran. Only 1,159 copies sold during the first year. Surprisingly, the sales doubled the following year, and again the year after that. Since then total sales have risen at a phenomenal rate—from 12,000 in 1935 to 111,000 in 1961 to 240,000 in 1964, and by now it is the all-time best-seller of the prestigious publishing house of Alfred A. Knopf, Inc. It has earned millions of dollars in royalties.

Nobody can understand the book's success, really. Book reviewer Stefan Kanfer wrote in the New York *Times Magazine* section in 1972, "of all the limp, mucid hooey now being sold without a prescription, 'The Prophet' is the most blatant and outrageous." But that is not the opinion of the millions of college kids who have bought and are still buying the book, with no need for advertising or reviews (though reviews appear perennially). A thin little volume of around 100 pages, the book concerns Almustafa, the Prophet, who bids the people of mythical Orphalese farewell after a 12-year sojourn in their land, and gives pronouncements on love, giving, food and drink, sorrow and joy, children, clothes and housing, buying and selling, crime and punishment, marriage, prayer, pleasure, beauty, religion, and death. In fact, it touches all bases, which may account for its universal appeal. It is often given as a gift to widows and orphans. But mainly it is the younger generation that has taken the book to its heart.

It wasn't until after his death in 1931 that Gibran returned to his beloved Bsherri. Thousands of mourners from Eastern and Western religions followed his funeral procession up the Lebanese hillside to the final burying place at Mar-Sakees Monastery. Gibran had died too soon to reap most of the harvest of *The Prophet*'s success, and the legacy he left Bsherri of the royalties from seven of his books didn't seem too important at the time. But the rapidly increasing bounty to the town, now up to nearly $1,000,000 a year, is what corrupted the town.

The feuds springing from differences over the administration of Gibran's legacy reached such proportions as to affect the national economy of Lebanon. The town dissolved into political, legal, and physical fighting for control of the money. Members of the leading families were named to a committee to administer the money. Soon political power and kickbacks began to accrue to committee members. Families split apart in the clamor to win a committee position. Age-old feuds, especially between the village's two main clans—the Keyrouz and the Tawks—gained fury, and at least two deaths resulted. Ultimately the two largest families, each with about 1,500 members, set up rival committees.

To add to the confusion, Gibran's sister Marianna (who died at the age of 94 in Boston) sought in 1946 to win control of the copyrights as each one came due for renewal. Knopf promptly began depositing all royalties in the registry of the

U. S. District Court, pending the outcome of the litigation. Its funds cut off, the dominant Bsherri committee retained George G. Shiya, a Wall Street lawyer of Lebanese extraction, as legal counsel. The case worked its tortuous way through the courts and finally, in 1964, judgment was rendered in favor of the committee, and the decision was eventually upheld by the U. S. Supreme Court. By the time the case was closed, the royalties on deposit with the court amounted to $831,789.23. By court order Shiya was awarded 25 percent of the committee's net share of the renewal copyrights as his legal fee.

In 1967 the Lebanese government threw out both competing committees handling the money and took over management of the estate itself. Though the village had received an estimated $1,000,000, it had little to show for the money except $200,000 worth of real estate investments. The bulk of the money had disappeared, and almost no records had been kept. When the government took over, Bsherri's warring elements finally made peace. A new committee was elected, this time with two members from each family and another member to represent residents who belong to no major family. One hundred Bsherri students have received scholarships or interest-free loans, a music academy has been opened, and two new schools and a mobile medical clinic came into being.

Here is Gibran's simple and well-meaning little will that started all the commotion:

> In the event of my death I wish that whatever money or securities Mr. Edgar Speyer has been gracious enough to hold for me should go to my sister Mary K. Gibran, who lives now at 76 Tyler Street, Boston, Mass.
>
> There are also 40 (forty) shares of the Fifty-one West Tenth Street Studio Association Stock lying in my safe deposit box with the Bank of Manhattan Trust Company, 31 Union Square, New York. These shares are also to go to my sister.

There are in addition to the foregoing 2 (two) bank books of the West Side Savings Bank, 422 Sixth Avenue, New York, which I have with me in my studio. I wish that my sister would take this money to my home town of Bechari, Republic of Lebanon, and spend it upon charities.

The royalties on my copyrights, which copyrights I understand can be extended upon request by my heirs for an additional period of twenty-eight years after my death, are to go to my home town.

Everything found in my studio after my death, pictures, books, objects of art, etcetera go to Mrs. Mary Haskell Mines, now living at 24 Gaston Street West, Savannah, Georgia, but I would like to have Mrs. Mines send all or any part of these things to my home town should she see fit to do so.

The will was dated March 13, 1930, and was witnessed by Lina Peck and Henry Lorch.

Chapter 15

A Will with Foresight

Benjamin Franklin expressed his gratitude to the cities of Boston, Massachusetts, and Philadelphia, Pennsylvania, and his desire to be useful to them even after his death, by bequeathing each city one thousand pounds sterling in trust, to be invested and used according to his explicit instructions in his will.

At the end of the first century, in accordance with the will, each city skimmed off $500,000 for public works. Today each city has a fund running into millions.

The will called for the termination of the bequests in 1991, and both cities will then be able to apply the residue to the cost of running the city governments.

These bequests to the cities of Boston and Philadelphia were not in Franklin's original will, dated July 17, 1788, but were made in a codicil dated June 23, 1789. Here are Franklin's actual words in which he made the bequests:

> In my will I bequeathed two thousand pounds to the State for the purpose of making Schuylkill River navigable. But understanding since that such a sum will do but little towards accomplishing such a work, and that the project is not likely to be undertaken for many years to come, and having entertained another idea that I hope may be more extensively useful, I do hereby revoke and annul that bequest and direct that the Certificates I have for what remains due to me that salary be sold towards raising the sum of five thousand pounds sterling to be disposed of as I am now about to order.

It has been an opinion that he who receives an estate from his ancestors is under some kind of obligation to transmit the same to their posterity. This obligation does not lie on me, who never inherited a shilling from any ancestor or relation: I shall however, if it is not diminished by some accident before my death, leave a considerable estate among my descendents and relations. The above observation is made merely as some apology to my family for making bequests that do not appear to have any immediate relation to their advantage.

I was born in Boston, New England, and owe my first instructions in literature to the free grammar schools established there. I have therefore already considered these schools in my will. But I am also under obligations to the state of Massachusetts for having unasked appointed me formerly their agent in England with a handsome salary which continued some years and altho I accidentally lost in their service by transmitting Governor Hutchinson's Letters much more than the amount of what they gave me, I do not think that ought in the least to diminish my gratitude.

I have considered that among artisans good apprentices are most likely to make good citizens; and having myself been bred to a manual art, printing, in my native town and afterwards assisted to set up my business in Philadelphia by kind loans of money from two friends. Their money was the foundation of my fortune and of all the utility that may be ascribed to me. I wish to be useful even after my death, if possible, in forming and advancing other young men that may be serviceable to their country in both those towns.

To this end, I devote two thousand pounds sterling which I give one thousand thereof to the inhabitants of Boston, Massachusetts, and the other thousand to the inhabitants of the city of Philadelphia, in trust to and for the uses, interests and purposes hereinafter mentioned and declared.

The said sum of one thousand pounds sterling, if accepted by the inhabitants of the town of Boston, shall be managed under the direction of the Select Men united with their Ministers of the oldest Episcopalian, Congregational and Presbyterian Churches in that town who are to let out the same upon interest at five per cent per annum to such married artificers, under the age of twenty-five years, as have served an apprenticeship in the said town, and faithfully fulfilled the duties required in their indentures, so as to obtain a good moral character from at least two respectable citizens who are willing to become their sureties in a bond with the applicants for the repayment of the money so lent with interest according to the terms hereinafter prescribed. All which bonds are to be taken for Spanish milled dollars or the value thereof in current gold coin. And they shall keep a bound book or books wherein shall be entered those names of those who shall apply for and receive the benefit of this institution and of their sureties together with the sums lent, the dates, and other necessary and proper records respecting the business and concerns of this institution. And as these loans are intended to assist young married artificers in setting up their business they are to be proportioned by the discretion of the managers so as not to exceed sixty pounds sterling to one person, nor to be less than fifteen pounds. And if the numbers of appliers so entitled should be so large so that the sum will not suffice to afford to each as much as might otherwise not be improper, the proportion to each shall be diminished, so as to afford to every one some assistance. These aids may therefore be small at first; but as the capital increases by the accumulated interest, they will be more ample. And in order to save as many as possible in their turn, as well as to make the repayment of the principal borrowed more easy, each borrower shall be obliged to pay with the yearly interest, one tenth part of the principal, which sums of principal and interest so paid in shall again be let out to fresh borrowers. And as it is presumed that there will always be found in Boston virtuous and benevolent citizens, willing to bestow a part of their time in doing good to the rising generation, by superintending and managing this institution gratis, it is hoped that no part of the money will at any time lie dead or be diverted to other purposes and be continually augmenting by the interest; in which case they may in time be more than the occasions in Boston shall require and then some may be spared to the neighboring or other towns in the state of Massachusetts who may desire to have it, such towns engaging to pay punctually the interest and the portions of the principal annually to the inhabitants of the town of Boston.

If this plan is executed and succeeds as projected without interruption for one hundred years, the sum will then be one hundred and thirty one thousand pounds of which I would have the managers of the donation to the town of Boston then lay out at their discretion one hundred thousand pounds in public works which may be judged of most general utility to the inhabitants such as fortifications, bridges, aqueducts, public buildings, baths, pavements or whatever may make living in the town more convenient to all people and render it more agreeable to strangers, resorting thither for health or a temporary residence. The remaining thirty one thousand pounds I would have continued to be let out on interest in the manner above directed for another hundred years, as I hope it will have been found that the insti-

tution has had a good effect on the conduct of youth
and been of service to many worthy characters and
useful citizens. At the end of this second term, if no
unfortunate accident has prevented the operation,
the sum will be four millions and sixty one thousand
pounds sterling of which I leave one million sixty-one
thousand pounds, to the disposition of the inhabitants
of the town of Boston and three millions to the disposition of the government of the state, not presum-
ing to carry my views farther.

All the directions herein given respecting the disposition and management of the donation to the inhabitants of Boston, I would have observed respecting that to the inhabitants of Philadelphia only as
Philadelphia incorporated. I request the Corporation
of the City to undertake the management agreeable
to the said directors and I do hereby vest them with
fair and ample powers for that purpose and having
considered that the covering its ground plot with
buildings and pavements which carry off most of
the rain and prevent its soaking into the earth and
renewing and purifying the springs, whence the water
of the wells must gradually grow worse, and in time
be unfit for use, as I find has happened in all old cities,
I recommend that at the end of the first hundred
years, if not done before, the corporation of the city
employ a part of the hundred thousand pounds in
bringing, by pipes, the water of Wissahickon Creek
into the town, so as to supply the inhabitants, which I
apprehend may be done without great difficulty, the
level of that creek being much above that of the city,
and may be made higher by a dam. I also recommend
making the Schuylkill completely navigable. At the
end of the second hundred years, I would have the
disposition of the four million and sixty one thousand
pounds divided between the inhabitants of the city
of Philadelphia and the government of Pennsylvania,

in the same manner as herein directed with respect to
that of the inhabitants of Boston and the government
of Massachusetts.

It is my desire that this institution should take place
and begin to operate within one year after my decease; for which purpose due notice should be pub-
lickly given previous to the aspiration of that year,
that those for whose benefit this establishment is
intended may make their respective applications.
And I hereby direct my Executors, the survivors or
survivor of them within six months after my decease
to pay over the said sum of two thousand pounds
sterling to such persons as shall be duly appointed
by the Select Men of Boston and the Corporation of
Philadelphia to receive and take charge of their respective sums of one thousand pounds each for the
purposes aforesaid.

Considering the accidents to which all human affairs and projects are subject in such a length of time,
I have perhaps too much flattered myself with a vain
fancy that these dispositions, if carried into execution, will be continued without interruption and have
the effects proposed. I hope however that if the inhabitants of the two cities should not think fit to undertake the execution, they will at least accept the
offer of these donations, as a mark of my good will,
a token of my gratitude and a testimony of my ear-
nest desire to be useful to them even after my departure. I wish indeed that they may both undertake
to endeavour the execution of the project; because,
I think that tho' unforeseen difficulties may arise,
expedients will be found to remove them, and the
scheme be found practicable. If one of them accepts
the money with the conditions, and the other refuses,
my wish then is that both sums be given to the inhabitants of the city accepting the whole to be ap-
plied to the same purposes and under the same regu-

lations, directed for the separate parts; and if both
refuse, the money of course remains in the mass of
my estate and is to be disposed of therewith according to my will made the seventeenth of July 1788.

The only items of particular interest in Franklin's original
will are these:

To my son William Franklin late Governor of the
Jerseys I give and devise all the lands I hold or have
a right to in the Province of Nova Scotia, to hold to
him his heirs and assigns forever. I also give to him
all my books and papers which he has in his possession and all debts standing against him on my account books willing that no payment for nor restitu-
tion of the same be required of him by my Executors:
the part he acted against me in the late war, which
is of public notoriety, will account for my leaving
him no more of an estate he endeavoured to deprive
me of.

The King of France's picture set with four hundred and eight diamonds, I give to my daughter Sarah
Bache; requesting however that she would not form
any of those diamonds into ornaments either for herself or daughters and thereby introduce or coun-
tenance the expensive vain and useless fashion of
wearing jewels in this country; and that those immediately connected with the picture may be pre-
served with the same.

Chapter 16

President ... Dictator ... Emperor ... King

According to his will, former President Harry S Truman left an estate estimated at $610,000, his personal property accounting for $600,000 of it, and his real property for the other $10,-000. The will left the bulk of the estate to Truman's widow, Bess, and his daughter, Margaret Truman Daniel, stipulating that those two share equally in the estate except for the automobiles and personal items at the Truman home in Independence, which go to Mrs. Truman. A trust fund was set up to provide Mrs. Truman with income for life, aside from the $20,000-a-year pension she receives from the federal government as the widow of a former President.

Originally drawn January 14, 1959, and amended October 23, 1961 and November 4, 1967, the will lists $18,005 in bequests, plus a grant of land to Grandview Masonic Lodge as a site for a lodge hall.

The four nephews and one niece of Truman and the two nieces and one nephew of Mrs. Truman receive $1,000 each. Fifteen grandnephews and grandnieces each receive $500. One grandnephew, John Ross Truman, was bequeathed only $5 because at the time the will was drawn he was a seminarian and had taken a vow of poverty.

Rose Conway, Truman's personal secretary, receives $1,000. Anne Smith, Frances M. Williams, and Mary Jo Nick, secretaries in his library, receive $500 each.

The will begins with Truman declaring that all of his presidential papers, with some exceptions, become the property of the people of the United States and will be housed in the

Truman Library in Independence "subject to the right of the archivist of the United States" to change the location.

Even the wording on his tombstone was dictated by President Truman. The will stipulates that the grave marker carry a simple list of eight important dates in his life. The slab, level with the ground, is to cover the graves of both Truman and his wife. Those eight dates to be recorded on it are the dates of his own birth, his marriage, his daughter Margaret's birth, and the dates of taking office during his political career—as a judge twice, as senator, as Vice President, and as President twice.

Another President of the United States, Zachary Taylor, was not as clever, either legally or financially, as President Truman. President Taylor died intestate, and the only clue to his financial status was a list of his goods, chattels, and personal estate, an inventory witnessed July 23, 1850, by J. H. Eaton. The list follows:

1 close carriage (nearly new)	$600.00
1 close carriage (much used)	150.00
1 pair of carriage horses	650.00
1 set double harness	100.00
1 lot of coine, assorted	577.00
2 milch cows	45.00
1 lot of tea, 62 lbs.	57.00
1 lot of butter, 320 lbs.	73.00
10 canvassed hams	10.00
1 lot small stores	14.00
1 lot sugar, coffee & candles	19.00
	$2295.00

President Taylor also had $3,893.34 cash in the bank at the time of his death, 100 shares of Western Bank valued at $2,000, and a sum due from the U. S. Treasury on account of savings as President of $407.60.

No will was ever filed. Letters of administration were issued to Wm. W. Bliss on July 20, 1850.

Franklin Delano Roosevelt's estate was estimated at $1,100,-
000. He directed that he and his wife be buried in the garden
of his Hyde Park property with a simple stone erected over
the graves. He bequeathed the rector of St. James Church in
Hyde Park the sum of $5,000 to be added to the cemetery
fund and used for the upkeep of the family burial lots. The
Georgia Warm Springs Foundation was bequeathed all of the
real estate located in Meriwether County, Georgia, with all
the buildings and improvements thereon.

Each person in Roosevelt's employ whose salaries or wages
were being paid by him personally received $100 in the will.
All the remaining estate was to be held in trust by James
Roosevelt and Basil O'Connor, jointly, and the bulk of this
trust was to benefit his widow and children.

Eleanor Roosevelt was given first choice in selecting whatever she wanted from Roosevelt's personal possessions (except the property bequeathed to Georgia Warm Springs
Foundation), and was to notify the executors within six
months, in writing, of which articles she had selected. Whatever was not chosen by Eleanor was then to be selected by
the children living at the time of Roosevelt's death or by his
executors for the issue then living of any deceased child or
children, provided what was selected would not exceed one
fifth the total value of the personal property. Such selections
should be made by unanimous agreement of the children, and
the executors should be notified of the selections made within
three months. The selections were to be made by the children
in the order of their seniority. Whatever was not selected by
anyone was to be left in the Hyde Park house, which was
given to the government of the United States, and was to be
offered as a gift to the U. S. government for display at the
Franklin D. Roosevelt Library or at the main house. Anything
not wanted by the children *or* the government was to be sold
by the executors at public or private sales.

Here is a stipulation in the will that will interest those who
read Elliott Roosevelt's book, *An Untold Story: The Roosevelts*

of Hyde Park, revealing the intimate relationship between his father and Marguerite ("Missy") LeHand:

During the lifetime of my wife the Trustees shall pay out of the remaining one half of her income of the trust fund to or for the account of my friend, Marguerite A. LeHand, such sum or sums at such time or times and in such manner as my Trustees, in their sole discretion, shall deem necessary and reasonable to discharge expenses incurred or which may be incurred by or for the said Marguerite A. LeHand for medical attention, care and treatment during her lifetime. The Trustees are also authorized, but not directed, to pay out of the said remaining one half of the net income of the trust fund to or for the account of the said Marguerite A. LeHand, during the lifetime of my wife, such sum or sums not exceeding a total of $1,000 per annum, at such time or times and in such manner as my Trustees, in their sole discretion, shall determine for maintenance and living expenses of Marguerite A. LeHand.

If Marguerite A. LeHand should survive both my wife and myself, then upon the death of my wife or upon my death if my wife shall not have survived me, the Trustees shall set apart from the principal of the trust fund such amount as they, in their sole discretion, shall deem necessary to carry out the provisions of this Paragraph and shall hold such principal upon a separate and independent trust and pay out the income and/or the principal thereof to or for the account of Marguerite LeHand in the amounts and at the time or times and in the manner and for the purposes hereinabove provided. Upon the death of Marguerite LeHand, the Trustees shall assign, convey, transfer, pay over and distribute any principal then remaining in such trust fund, together with any income thereon, in equal shares to my children then

living and the issue then living of any deceased children of mine, such issue to take per stirpes and not
per capita.

Here is the will of Adolf Hitler:

Although during the years of struggle I believed
that I could not undertake the responsibility of marriage, now before the end of my life, I have decided
to take as my wife the woman (Eva Braun) who,
after many years of true friendship, came to this city,
almost already besieged, of her own free will in order
to share my fate.

She will go to her death with me at her own wish
as my wife. This will compensate us both for what
we both lost through my work in the service of my
people.

My possessions, insofar as they are worth anything,
belong to the party, or, if this no longer exists, to the
state. If the state, too, is destroyed, there is no need
for any further instructions on my part. The paintings
in the collections bought by me during the years
were never assembled for private purposes but solely
for the establishment of a picture gallery in my home
town of Linz on the Danube.

It is my most heartfelt wish that this will should
duly be executed. As executor I appoint my most
faithful party comrade, Martin Bormann. He receives
full legal authority to make all decisions. He is permitted to hand over to my relatives everything that is
of value as a personal memento or is necessary for
maintaining a petit-bourgeois standard of living,
especially to my wife's mother and my faithful fellow
workers of both sexes who are well known to him.

The chief of these are my former secretaries, Frau
Winter, etc., who helped me for many years by their
work.

My wife and I choose to die in order to escape the shame of overthrow or capitulation. It is our wish for our bodies to be cremated immediately on the place where I have performed the greater part of my daily work during twelve years of service to my people.

Berlin, 29 April, 1400 hours.

A. Hitler

WITNESSES: Martin Bormann, Dr. Joseph Goebbels, Nicolaus von Buelow.

Once the most towering figure in European history, despite his small stature, and crowned Emperor of France, Napoleon died stripped of all power, possessions, and money. Only one thing he created lived on: his "Code Napoleon." The code is a system of laws promulgated under his order and written by the most eminent French jurists, and is a concise outline of judicial procedure and includes a precise set of rules for the laws of inheritance.

Napoleon wrote his own will three weeks before his death on April 15, 1821, at St. Helena. The official cause of death was cancer. There are still those who choose to believe the rumor that he was poisoned.

The opening lines of Napoleon's will are known to most Frenchmen by heart: "It is my wish that my ashes may repose on the banks of the Seine, in the midst of the French people, whom I have loved so well."

It continues, "I have always had reasons to be pleased with my dearest wife Marie Louise. I retain for her to my last moment the most tender sentiments. I beseech her to watch, in order to preserve my son from the snares which yet environ his infancy.

"I recommend to my son never to forget that he was born a French Prince, and never to allow himself to become an instrument in the hands of the Triumvirs who oppress the nations of Europe: he ought never to fight against France, or

to injure her in any manner: he ought to adopt my motto—
'Everything for the French People.'

"I die prematurely, assassinated by the English oligarchy
—the English nation will not be slow in avenging me."

It was 1840 before the remains of Napoleon were brought
back to Paris and placed in Les Invalides, where they now
repose.

Nobody except the inheritors and the lawyer will ever know
the exact disposition of the estate of the Duke of Windsor,
once King of England. Now that he is dead he has been ac-
corded a royal privilege, few of which he received during his
life in exile. This royal privilege is that the way in which he
disposed of his small £7,845 English estate will remain a secret. One wonders who among all his relatives and friends who
turned their backs on him when he abdicated to marry the
woman he loved the Duke remembered fondly enough to bequeath them his paltry holdings in England and Wales. When
he abdicated in 1936, the Duke transferred the private royal
estates in Britain to his brother King George VI. Ostensibly,
then, he left England fairly broke. Yet when he died he left
a fortune estimated at $2.5 million in France, with his Duchess
as sole legatee. He denied during an interview that he received
an income from the Crown. "I inherited absolutely nothing,"
he said.

One can only assume that the Duke amassed his fortune
through careful investments and the guidance of friends. There
were definitely many fringe benefits to being a former King
in exile. For instance, he and the Duchess were given, at very
small cost, a choice tract of land in Marbella, with the hope
that this maneuver would attract other land buyers, which of
course it did. They never built on the property, and eventually
sold it at a very high price.

Peter Karageorgevich, formerly King Peter II of Yugoslavia,
left a two-page will which, according to the New York *Times*,
included "such curious provisions that some of his family sus-

pect it might have been drafted when he was of unsound mind." The will was executed four months before his death from a combination of ailments including what the death certificate listed as a "chronic brain injury," which had endured for three months. Probated less than a week after Peter died and three days before the death certificate was filed, the will refers to his wife as "Alexandra" and is signed in an almost illegible hand.

In addition to the mysteries surrounding the will, the death certificate contained several inaccuracies. That document listed him as "Peter Petrovich" and states he "never married" and had no surviving spouse. Furthermore, it said his mother's maiden name was unknown although, in fact, she was Princess Marie of Romania, Queen Victoria's granddaughter.

Technically, Peter became King at age eleven, when his father, Alexander I, was assassinated. However, Prince Paul, a cousin of Alexander I, ruled the country through a Council of Regents until forces backing Peter seized control in 1941. Only two weeks later the new King was forced to flee the country when the Nazis occupied much of Yugoslavia.

Peter established an exile regime in Britain, but when Marshal Tito gained control in 1945, Peter never returned. He lived in the United States for a number of years, and died in Denver.

The estate is valued in excess of $2 million. A total of $2 million was deposited in Swiss banks after Peter fled the country in 1941. However, according to an attorney for the estate, the Swiss bankers would not let the ex-King withdraw the money because they did not recognize him as head of state.

Peter left $5,000 to his only child, Alexander Karadjordjevich, who now resides in England. "He has been well taken care of my [sic] various trusts and gifts," the will said.

Seventy-five percent of his residuary estate went to his wife, who lives in Venice, Italy. She was Princess Alexandra, niece of King George II of Greece.

The remainder of the residuary estate went to the "Liberty Eastern Serbian Orthodox Monastery, Liberty (actually Libertyville), Illinois," where the will directed he be buried, "not withstanding any other desires of my family."

The only living person named in both the will and the death certificate was Mitzi Lowe, the testator's "friend and benefactor," who was named executrix. She is also the person specified on the death certificate as the "informant" presumably responsible for the inaccuracies in the certificate mentioned earlier.

Peter is the only European King ever to be buried in this country.

Chapter 17

Seven Instant Millionaires

The will that resulted in seven instant millionaires was that of Eleanor Medill ("Cissy") Patterson, who was publisher of the Washington *Times-Herald* at the time of her death. The lucky seven were editors and executives of the paper, and she hadn't really meant for them to become instant millionaires; she'd meant for them to continue operating the paper.

To understand this bequest, what led up to it and what followed afterward, one must understand Cissy Patterson herself. The newspaper business was the source of her wealth and the joy of her life. Her brother Joseph Medill Patterson and her cousin Robert Rutherford McCormick made their grandfather's Chicago *Tribune* into one of the nation's most successful newspapers; then brother Joe founded the New York *Daily News*, which reached an all-time peak in circulation.

Cissy liked the idea of being in newspaper work herself, but the chance didn't come until after the death of her second husband, Elmer Schlesinger. Up until that time she had been a bit busy dusting off the impecunious Polish count, Joseph Gizcyka, whom she'd married at nineteen; spending half a million dollars getting their daughter Felicia away from him after he kidnaped the child; traveling ceaselessly; enjoying the social life of Washington; and writing two novels.

By the time Schlesinger died, Felicia had married columnist Drew Pearson, and so Cissy was alone—and restless. She wanted to write, and something to write *in*, so she tried to persuade William Randolph Hearst, Sr., to sell his ailing Washington *Herald* to her. The circulation of the paper was only sixty thousand and in trouble, but Hearst didn't want to sell. Instead, he appointed Cissy as its editor at $15,000 a year —a pittance compared to the million-dollar-a-year income she was deriving from her share of her brother's papers.

The fact that Cissy arrived at her newly decorated chintzy office in riding habit or evening dress, conveyed in her chauffeured Cadillac or Deusenberg, and accompanied by a flock of yapping French poodles, fooled some people into thinking she did not take the job seriously. But they were wrong: She did work very hard at her job. To convince her managing editor she was willing to cover more than society, Cissy assumed the disguise of a jobless maid and visited Washington's relief agencies collecting material for a series. She even planned to spend the night at a mission in Washington's Skid Row, taking along, of course, her own bed coverings, silk nightie, robe, and toiletries. However, she never had an opportunity to interview the bums she had hoped to see the next morning. The minute she lay down she spotted a cockroach on the ceiling, and fled the mission with her mink coat thrown over her nightie.

As time went on, and as fresh talent was imported to help run the paper, advertisers began to take an interest in the newly exciting *Herald*, it began doing better, and Cissy was made publisher.

To some of her employees Cissy seemed a martinet; to others, a real sport. She cruelly fired some for almost no reason. Yet one night when she got a drunken call around 3 A.M. from a group of employees having a farewell party for Ray Helgesen, she invited the entire party over to her fabulous mansion on Dupont Circle, roused the help, ordered out the good champagne and whiskey, had supper served, and laughed and danced with the drunks.

Cissy's dual personality showed itself in other ways, too. She was a violent antivivisectionist; yet she shot a horse that threw her. She fired a new photo editor she had just hired from Boston because he printed an unflattering picture of her on his first day at work. (On the train bearing him miserably back to Boston, he glanced out and saw his wife and children on a train taking them to join him in Washington.) On the other side of the coin, she immediately checked out of a hotel in Miami when one of her Jewish employees was not allowed to join her in that restricted hotel. Only the day before, she had ensconced herself in the hotel for a month's stay, with her mountain of trunks, bags, dogs, and trappings.

In 1937 Cissy managed to buy both the *Herald* and the *Times,* published in the same building, at a total cost of $1,557,-500. She combined the two papers into the *Washington Times-Herald,* and her career came into full flower.

This exciting maverick, with her waist-length red hair, her warm or cold brown eyes (depending upon whom they were focusing), her love of life, and her fire, died at the age of sixty-three while reading a book in bed at Dower House, her Maryland retreat.

Cissy's will reflects her love of her newspaper. Her original will left her newspaper to eight loyal employees: William Shelton, general manager; Frank Waldrop, editor-in-chief; Edmund P. Jewell, advertising director; Michael Flynn, supervising managing editor; H. A. (Happy) Robinson, circulation manager; Irving Belt, mechanical superintendent; Mason Peters, night managing editor; and C. B. Porter. But true to form, Cissy changed her mind about Mr. Porter before her death and wrote a codicil eliminating him.

Slow mails and Cissy's vacillation caused those seven to receive their bonanza. Cissy had just about decided that her niece Alicia Patterson Guggenheim, Joe's daughter and wife of multimillionaire Harry F. Guggenheim, was the person best fitted to carry on with the *Times-Herald,* and was exchanging a series of letters with her cousin "Bertie" regarding changing the will when she died, without having time to have her proposed new will legalized.

When she chose those seven as beneficiaries, Cissy hoped they would carry on with the newspaper, but being a realist, she inserted a clause that they could not sell it without the consent of all beneficiaries. She also inserted a clause that "in the event of the death of any such beneficiary after his interest has vested but before distribution takes place, his interest shall pass to his personal representative." To forestall the possibility of that latter eventuality, the seven heirs rather quickly sold out to Bertie McCormick for *Tribune* stock and cash. The seven inheritors each got $1.5 million.

Cissy's daughter Felicia, with whom she was never too close, received Cissy's Port Washington estate, numerous personal items, and $25,000 a year for life, but she wasn't happy with her bequest. She contested the will on the grounds her mother was demented. The seven heirs paid her off to the tune of $400,000.

Probably the most surprised inheritor was Cissy's Maryland neighbor Ann Bowie Smith, who received Dower House. Ann had shared Cissy's love of flowers, and disgruntled noninheritors decided Cissy wanted her country estate to go to someone who would continue to take care of the orchids she adored. Cissy had several greenhouses full of them, and they were the first stop on her tours of inspection with guests.

The American Red Cross was the happy recipient of Cissy's mansion on Dupont Circle.

The most endearing part of her will was Cissy's stipulation that money would continue to be sent regularly to several down-and-out friends whom she had quietly been supporting for years.

What happened to the lucky seven inheritors? All but one stayed rich. That one blew his money on a yacht and a couple of grabby wives. Three are now dead. One, Happy Robinson, is still working, at the age of eighty-eight, on Cissy's rival newspaper, the Washington *Post,* for the princely sum of $1 a year. He doesn't need the money, but he loves the work.

Cissy's ex-son-in-law, Drew Pearson, did not take a cue from his former mother-in-law and draw up a legal will in a lawyer's office. He wrote out a new will on hotel stationery whenever the mood moved him. It moved him at least seven times, because seven hand-written, unwitnessed, unalike wills were found after his death. The problem was establishing which was the last and most meaningful one, and it took years to straighten out his estate, according to famous Washington lawyer Edward Bennett Williams.

Chapter 18

Wills Dictating Funerals, Wakes,
and Disposition of the Remains

A few testators are concerned about the disposition of their remains and the type of wake and funeral to be held for them. The most popular disposition of remains is cremation and the scattering of the ashes over some favorite spot—usually the city in which the deceased lived, the ocean, or some happily remembered vacation spot. Honolulu gets a lot of ashes scattered over it—not an easy task when one remembers how hard it is to open a window in an airplane. The wife of a Hollywood producer asked so many friends to scatter his ashes over Honolulu, as requested in his will, she lost track of the ashes and doesn't know to this day where they ended up.

The wife of a once-famous vaudevillian wanted him to keep her ashes on the dresser near his bed. He complied with that wish, but the new wife he married three months later isn't exactly enchanted with the idea.

A disgruntled golfer, whose ball always seemed to end up in a certain sandtrap on the golf course where he always played, willed that his ashes be placed in that sandtrap.

Winston Churchill left a complete blueprint for his own funeral, which was carried out to the letter.

The late great rock singer Janis Joplin left the amount of $2,500 to be spent on a farewell party for her after her death at her favorite pub, the Lion's Share in San Anselmo, California, where she had often sung. Since the pub only serves beer and wine, it took all night for the invited guests on her list to drink up the bequest. Movie star Wayne Morris had a similar idea. In his will he left $100 to be spent at his funeral for "booze and canapes," and then added, "make it $300 because I don't want my friends to go away sober or serious."

A socialite lady in Washington went even further. She specified that she was to be present at that farewell party, and was. The wake was in the form of a cocktail party in her home, with the deceased's favorite orchestra playing in the ballroom. The deceased was half lying on a chaise with a glass of champagne in her dead hand and an undertaker's Mona Lisa smile on her lips, while her friends danced around her.

In the late thirties an Italian merchant of Turin named Carmelo Giannattei left his whole estate, estimated at about $10,000, to his brother Adolfo, with the stipulation that Adolfo must recite prayers on his tomb at 9 A.M. every morning. If he should fail even once to do so, the entire estate would automatically pass to his other two brothers, Angelo and Ricardo. Angelo and Ricardo mounted guard on their dead brother's tomb to make sure Adolfo did his duty. For eight consecutive months, through rain, snow, or sunshine, Adolfo punctually arrived at the cemetery and mumbled some prayers on Carmelo's tomb. Then one January he did not appear for two weeks in succession. The two other brothers were there every day, however, making happy note of Adolfo's absence. They brought more witnesses to the cemetery to confirm Adolfo's defection, then contacted their lawyers to claim Carmelo's heritage. Adolfo's claim that he had been sick carried no weight.

Miss Florence Groff, the daughter of Professor William T. Groff, a noted archaeologist from Cincinnati, was herself an archaeologist, writer, and student of languages—she spoke thirty-six dialects. Her father and brother were buried in Greece, and her mother was buried in Egypt. They just happened to be in those far-off places excavating when they died. Miss Groff had just one ambition in life—and death. She spelled it out in her will. She wanted the bodies of her family brought back and buried with her in her family's 420-square-foot lot in Spring Grove Cemetery, Cincinnati. Furthermore, she wanted an Egyptian-type pyramid to be built to cover the entire lot. When Miss Groff died she was more than ninety years old, and lived in a half-finished house she had helped construct at Hastings-on-Hudson, New York. Among the litter found by police in the half-starved woman's shack were stocks, bonds, French coins, five bank books, Egyptian relics, and oil paintings. The estate was estimated at $40,000, after being depleted by long litigation and examinings.

Cemetery officials and the city fathers denied Miss Groff's request for such a huge pyramid, as it would not conform to the appearance of the rest of the cemetery. A compromise was finally reached, and $10,000 was allotted for the building of a type of pyramid. Two distant cousins who had contested the will got the rest. The family is buried all together at last, but the much-desired tomb of the Pharaohs is only a shadow of the one provided for in Miss Groff's will. It is six feet high and six feet square at its base, and is distinguished among the surrounding expensive monuments only by its odd shape.

Ervin Charles Putnam, of Denver, wanted to be sure he and his wife had flowers put on their graves, and left $1,000 for that purpose. The flowers were to be placed on the graves every Sunday and also on Christmas.

Charles W. Sonnenberg, of Baltimore, was equally unsure of the good intentions of his friends and relatives. He left $5,000 for weekly supplies of fresh flowers on his grave.

William Granville, an eccentric British clerk of the Treasury, made sure he would not be lonely in his grave. He left instructions in his will that 40 shillings be awarded to each of five poor boys under 16 on the anniversary of his death. To earn the bequest, the five boys were to recite the Lord's Prayer every February 15, with their hands on his gravestone.

A wealthy real estate man in Belgrade, Yugoslavia, named Lazar Kutovitch wrote in his will: "In death I wish to have the comforts which for so many years were denied to me in life. Therefore I am setting aside 100,000 dinars (about $2,000) to be buried sitting up in an armchair with a table, cigarettes, matches, and my first wife's photographs beside me." Kutovitch also provided $10,000 for the erection of a specially built Greek Orthodox church with a glass floor. He wished to be

embalmed in his comfortable position under the church so
that those who had known of his unhappiness in life could see
how restful he was when they came to pray. Even in death,
poor Kutovitch was denied the comforts that he lacked when
married to his nagging second wife. The authorities decided
his strange request was understandable but illegal. They buried
him in a cemetery after giving him an elaborate funeral in
keeping with his wealth.

Bernard Sunley, a British civil engineer and property developer, made sure his employees would remember him happily. He bequeathed $9,800 for the employees to enjoy a
banquet at his expense.

The will of the Marquis de Sade, after giving money and
possessions to Mme. Marie-Constance Reinelle in gratitude for
the care and friendship she gave him during his latter years,
was largely concerned with the disposition of his body after
his death. The will says:

> I absolutely forbid that my body be opened upon
> any pretext whatsoever. I urgently insist that it be
> kept a full forty-eight hours in the chamber where I
> shall have died, placed in a wooden coffin which shall
> not be nailed shut until the prescribed forty-eight
> hours have elapsed, at the end of which period the
> said coffin shall be nailed shut; during this interval a
> message shall be sent express to M. Le Normand,
> wood seller in Versailles, living at number 101, boule-
> vard de L'Égalite, requesting him to come in his own
> person, with a cart, to fetch my body away and to
> convey it under his own escort and in the said cart to
> the wood upon my property at Malmaison near
> Épernon, in the commune of Emance, where I would
> have it laid to rest, without ceremony of any kind,
> in the first copse standing to the right as the said wood
> is entered from the side of the old château by way of
> the broad lane dividing it. The ditch opened in this
> copse shall be dug by the farmer tenant of Malmaison

under M. Le Normand's supervision, who shall not
leave my body until after he has placed it in the said
ditch; upon this occasion he may, if he so wishes, be
accompanied by those among my kinsmen or friends
who without display or pomp of any sort whatsoever
shall have been kind enough to give me this last proof
of their attachment. The ditch once covered over,
above it acorns shall be strewn, in order that the spot
become green again, and the copse grown back thick
over it, the traces of my grave may disappear from
the face of the earth as I trust the memory of me
shall fade out of the minds of all men save nevertheless for those few who in their goodness have loved
me until the last and of whom I carry away a sweet
remembrance with me to the grave.

The will was dated January 30, 1806.

Actor Van Heflin's will, executed less than a month before
he died of a stroke, directed that his body be cremated, that
there be no funeral or memorial service of any kind or nature,
and that his ashes be strewn over the Pacific Ocean.

A great many people express the wish in their wills to be
buried on their own property. These requests are usually
turned down because of city ordinances. A relative few manage to find a loophole, however. The late great advertising
tycoon Schuyler ("Sky") Kudner sleeps peacefully on his beloved ranch in the West. Dr. Charles Mayo, founder of the
Mayo Clinic in Rochester, and his wife lie side by side under
their favorite big tree in their backyard.

Chapter 19
No Legal Jargon

John B. ("Jack") Kelly of Philadelphia, who was extremely popular and well known long before his daughter Grace focused the attention of the world on her family by marrying Prince Rainier of Monaco, displayed his buoyant spirit, his Irish sense of humor, and his avid interest in life—and death—when he dictated his will to his stenographer two months before he died of cancer in 1960, and signed it in green ink. The will has become a classic, and parts of it have been widely reprinted.

Kelly accumulated his fortune in the bricklaying business—a business that was to brand him not quite a gentleman when, as American sculling champion, he wanted to enter the sculling championship races at Henley, England. The excuse for barring him was that "he worked with his hands." Chagrined at this setback, Kelly sent his insignia green cap to King George V with a note saying he would have a son who would come back and win. Under the tutelage of Kelly and his beloved wife Margaret, a former physical education teacher, his son Jack, Jr., did win the Henley. When he stepped out of the scull on that great day, young Jack handed his green cap to his father and said, "Here, Dad, this belongs to you."

Kelly was the youngest of a large family of modest means. His oldest brother, Walter, became one of the most famous vaudevillians of his time with an act called "The Virginia Judge." Another brother, George, was a playwright who had three plays running on Broadway at once. Kelly's sister Mary was his favorite—the one who always helped and encouraged him.

Starting as an apprentice bricklayer, Kelly went on to become owner of his own large company, a big wheel in Democratic circles in Philadelphia, head of President Roosevelt's physical fitness program, and president of the Atlantic City Race Track.

Even as an apprentice bricklayer, Kelly spent all his spare time sculling at the social boat clubs along the river, and became so good at it he won the Olympic championship. He was greeted on his return from that feat by a private train chartered by the bricklayers' union to escort him back to Philadelphia, a big parade, and a banquet in his honor.

Though accustomed to fanfare, Kelly was unusually pleased over all the hoopla attending the wedding of his daughter Grace to Rainier. That day, and the day Jack, Jr., won the Henley, might have been the proudest moments of his life.

Kelly dictated his will without benefit of a lawyer. Though completely unorthodox, the will was carefully scrutinized by Kelly's lawyers and is perfectly legal. It is also warm, earthy, and charming. Here it is, with a few paragraphs regarding purely business matters deleted:

For years I have been reading Last Wills and Testaments, and I have never been able to clearly understand any of them at one reading. Therefore, I will attempt to write my own Will with the hope that it will be understandable and legal. Kids will be called "kids" and not "issue," and it will not be cluttered up with "parties of the first part," "per stirpes," "perpetuities," "quasijudicial," "to wit" and a lot of other terms that I am sure are only used to confuse those for whose benefit it is written.

This is my Last Will and Testament and I believe I am of sound mind. (Some lawyers will question this when they read my Will, however, I have my opinion of some of them, so that makes it even.) I revoke any and all previous Wills made before by me.

I give to my wife, Margaret, any interest I may own in any real estate I am using as a residence, either as a home or for vacations, at the time of my death, together with any insurance thereon. I also give to my wife any automobiles, furniture, silverware, chinaware, books, pictures, jewelry, clothing and other articles of household or personal use owned by me at my death, together with any insurance thereon. I would like my wife, Margaret, to give my son John Brendan Kelly, who will be known hereinafter by his rowing title of "Kell," all my personal belongings, such as trophies, rings, jewelry, watches, clothing and athletic equipment, except the ties, shirts, sweaters and socks, as it seems unnecessary to give him something of which he has already taken possession. If, however, any special trophy, such as medals, watches, etc., should be desired for a keepsake by Baba, Grace or Liz, this is to be decided by my wife, who is to be the sole judge.

Godfrey Ford has been with me over forty-five years, and has been a faithful and loyal servant. Therefore I want him to be kept in employment as long as he behaves himself well, making due allowances for minor errors of the flesh, if being slightly on the Casanova side is an error. I want my survivors to feel an obligation regarding his comfort and employment. In addition, I give him $1,000 outright. I have already turned over to him the bonds I bought for him at Christmas each year.

I give to Mary Trenwith, if she survives me, $1,000 as a reward for her faithful service while I was in training during my rowing days.

I wish to take full advantage of the marital deduction allowed with respect to the federal estate tax. If my wife, Margaret, survives me, therefore, I give my trustees, as a separate trust for her, a one-third share of the residue of my estate.

I give the balance of the residue of my estate in equal shares to my son Kell (John Brendan Kelly), my daughter Baba (Margaret Kelly Davis), my daughter Grace (Her Serene Highness, Princess Grace) and my daughter Liz (Elizabeth Anne Le-Vine). If any of my daughters does not survive me, her share shall pass equally to her children who survive me.

In the case of my daughters' husbands, they do not share and if any of my daughters die, her share goes to her children, or if there are no children, then that share goes back into my own children's fund. I don't want to give the impression that I am against sons-in-law—if they are the right type, they will provide for themselves and their families and what I am able to give my daughters will help pay the dress shop bills, which, if they continue as they started out, under the able tutelage of their mother, will be quite considerable.

I can think of nothing more ghastly than the heirs sitting around listening to some representative reading a Will. They always remind me of buzzards awaiting the last breath of the stricken. Therefore I will try to spare you that ordeal and let you read the Will before I go to my reward—whatever it will be. I do hope that it will never be necessary to go into Court over spoils, for to me the all-time low in family affairs is a court fight, in which I have seen families engage. If you cannot agree, I direct that the executor or trustees, as the case may be, shall decide all questions of administration or distribution, as the executor and trustees will be of my choosing or yours.

I will try to give each of you all I can during my life so that you will have money in your own right—in that way, you will not be wholly dependent on my bequest. I want you all to understand that U. S. Government Bonds are the best investment even if the return is small, and then comes Commonwealths and Municipals, that have never failed to meet their interest charges. As the years gather you will meet some pretty good salesmen who will try to sell you everything from stock in a copper or gold mine to some patent that they will tell you will bring you millions, but remember, that for every dollar made that way, millions have been lost. I have been taken by this same gentry but that was perhaps because I had to learn from experience—when my father died, my hopes were high, but the exchequer low, and the stock market was on the other side of the railroad tracks, as far as I was concerned.

To Kell, I want to say that if there is anything to this Mendelian theory, you will probably like to bet on a horse or indulge in other forms of gambling— so if you do, never bet what you cannot afford to lose and if you are a loser, don't plunge to try to recoup. That is wherein the danger lies. "There will be another deal, my son, and after that, another one." Just be moderate in all things and don't deal in excesses. (The girls can also take that advice.) I am not going to try to regulate your lives, as nothing is quite as boring as too many "don'ts." I am merely setting down the benefit of my experience, which most people will admit was rather broad, since it runs from Port Said to Hawaii, Miami Beach to South America.

I hereby nominate, constitute and appoint my son, John Brendan Kelly, and Provident Tradesmens Bank and Trust Company, as co-executors of this my Last Will and Testament. . . . I appoint my friend, John Morgan Davis, my wife, Margaret M. Kelly, and my son, John Brendan Kelly, to be the trustees under this my Will. I direct that John Edward Sheridan, Esquire, shall be retained as counsel for my estate.

I have written this Will in a lighter vein because I have always felt that Wills were so dreary that they might have been written by the author of "Inner Sanctum" and I can see no reason for it, particularly in my case. My family is raised and I am leaving enough so they can face life with a better than average start, financially.

As for me, just shed a respectful tear if you think I merit it, but I am sure that you are all intelligent enough not to weep all over the place. I have watched a few emotional acts at graves, such as trying to jump into it, fainting, etc., but the thoroughbreds grieve in the heart.

Not that my passing should occasion any "scenes" for the simple reason that life owes me nothing. I have ranged far and wide, have really run the gamut of life. I have known great sorrow and great joy. I had more than my share of success. Up to this writing my wife and children have not given me any heartaches, but on the contrary, have given me much happiness and a pardonable pride, and I want them to know I appreciate that. I worked hard in my early life, but I was well paid for that effort.

In this document I can only give you things, but if I had the choice to give you worldly goods or character, I would give you character. The reason I say that, is with character you will get worldly goods because character is loyalty, honesty, ability, sportsmanship and, I hope, a sense of humor.

If I don't stop soon, this will be as long as "Gone with the Wind," so just remember, when I shove off for greener pastures or whatever it is on the other side of the curtain, that I do it unafraid and if you must know, a little curious.

Chapter 20

The Start of a Billionaire

None of the biographers of Howard Hughes, Jr., and there will undoubtedly be many of them after he is gone, will be able to use the old cliché "he made it all on his own." Thanks to the wills of his father and mother, he had a good head start toward the building of his staggering financial empire. Via his parents' wills, Howard, Jr., received 75 percent of the stock of the Hughes Company, the value of which at that time was fixed at $660,000 by the federal taxing authorities. The balance of 25 percent was left to other relatives, but after a year's trading Howard succeeded in having the company buy the other 25 percent for $325,000, which made his shares the only shares outstanding and Howard the sole owner of the company.

Like his son, Howard, Sr., was also born with a silver spoon in his mouth. His father served as the president of a railroad, and later became a prominent judge in Missouri. After graduating from Harvard, Howard, Sr., obtained admission to the bar after only two years' study at the University of Iowa's law school. Craving more excitement than the life of a lawyer offered, Howard in 1909 went off to Texas, where he negotiated leases for oil companies as close as possible to big oil strikes. Some were very successful, some not. During one of the affluent periods, Howard married Allene Gano, a descendant of a French Huguenot family that traced its roots back to Charlemagne. At the end of a $50,000 European honeymoon Howard was broke and Allene was pregnant. A son, Howard Robard Hughes, Jr., was born to them on December 24, 1905. Drilling failures at Pierce Junction and Goose Creek, Texas, because the drills being used could not penetrate rock formation inspired Howard, Sr., and with an engineer, he developed a two-cone bit with 166 cutting edges. Taking this tool back to Goose Creek, he fastened it to the drilling rig, and within eleven hours it went through fourteen feet of hard rock, like cutting through cream cheese. The first Goose Creek gusher was brought in. He formed a partnership with Walter Sharp.

When World War I broke out, Hughes offered the tool to the War Department. After being rebuffed in this offer for some time, the Army finally agreed to set up arrangements for an official test. The test proved the capability of the tool without a shadow of a doubt, but because of all the red tape involved, not one ever got to France. However, Hughes did receive a letter from the Secretary of War thanking him for his patriotic effort on behalf of the United States.

Sharp died in 1917, and Hughes bought out his interest in their company for $325,000.

Howard, Sr., had many of the traits that his son later displayed. He was six feet three, handsome, and had an eye for beautiful women. On visits to Hollywood he preferred the company of beautiful female stars. They all noticed that he sat rather close to them and watched their lips as they talked, which indicates that he, like his son, was hard of hearing. His wife learned of his romance with actress Eleanor Boardman, and wrote him a note the night before she was to have an operation telling him she knew of the romance and forgave him. Allene must have had a premonition of death, as she died on the operating table. Though Hughes deeply mourned her passing and never married again, he was seen in public escorting models and actresses again, after a respectable period of mourning. In 1924, two years after Allene died, Hughes dropped dead of a heart attack while discussing business in his office.

Although he had recently prepared a new will, he hadn't gotten around to signing it, so the old will remained in force. It was a simple will:

To my wife Allene Hughes, ½ of the whole
To my son Howard Robard Hughes, Jr., ¼ of the
whole
To my father Felix T. Hughes, ¹⁄₁₂ of the whole
To my mother Jean Hughes, ¹⁄₁₂ of the whole
To my sister, Mrs. Herbert Witherspoon, ¹⁄₁₂ of the
whole

Because his sister had died, there was a memorandum at
the bottom that her share should go to his brother Felix.

The tax returns of husband and wife placed the total of the
estates at $660,000. Hughes' friend and biographer Albert B.
Gerber said the debt reductions claimed by the executors
to reduce taxes were indicative of the kind of life Hughes had
led. There were Brooks Brothers' bills for over $2,000 for all
manner of men's wear, and jewelers' bills exceeded $5,000.

Under Texas law, young Howard inherited his mother's
share, which made him ¾ owner of the Hughes Tool Company at the age of nineteen. He chafed at having members
of the family as partners. Again under Texas law, if a minor
could convince the court that he had the ability to handle his
own affairs, he could be declared competent to enter into
binding contracts. Going into the probate court, his disabili-
ties as a minor were removed, and thereafter, the Hughes Tool
Company bought out the other relatives, making him sole
owner.

The will of Howard Hughes, Jr., is certain to be much more
complex than that of his father. According to Noah Dietrich,
who was with Hughes for thirty-two years until Dietrich told
him off and quit, Hughes has already written several wills.
"Characteristic of Howard's proclivity for secrecy," says
Dietrich, he never permitted anyone, including his lawyer,
to see his will. In 1949 he decided to write a new will. He had
made various promises to Dietrich about including him and
other officers in his will, but there is no evidence he even had
one at that time. At any rate, he secured from Lloyd Wright,
his No. 1 lawyer, various typed paragraphs for different pur-

poses. "I was to be named as Chairman of the Board of Trustees for the Medical Foundation for which he had provided," said Dietrich of Hughes' will. "Imagine my surprise when Frye and Perelle each independently told me Hughes had so informed them. Such perfidy!

"Eventually his secretary, Nadine Henley and her staff typed five substitute pages for each page of the will. He then personally selected the pages he decided to use, stapled them together and had Nadine and her assistant Marion witness his signature, exposing the last page only to them. It supposedly reposes in a safety deposit box but, of course, he may even have destroyed it. On his death I can foresee a residency contest on the part of the States of Texas, California and Nevada with an effort to invalidate the will on the basis of incompetency."

Chapter 21

Buried Treasure

A frugal old tobacco-chewing, overall-wearing bachelor farmer in Maryland with the unlikely name of C. Herman Rabbitt never got his name in the paper and was never heard of by anyone except his neighbors and cattle dealers until he died on October 10, 1972, at the age of eighty-one. He might not have made the papers even then, though it was discovered he'd left an estate of between two and three million dollars, except for one rather startling fact: Over half a million of it was buried on the farm where he lived. Now old Herman is a legend—the stuff of folk songs. His whole life, so secret before, is now an open book, and his will is being madly contested—and all because a bank where he kept his savings failed during the Depression years, and he decided to bury his ready cash, to keep it safe.

Though he was generally considered tight-fisted and ornery, Rabbitt had the grudging respect of his friends and neighbors because he made it all on his own. He was such a shrewd bargainer in cattle, land, and horses, that he gradually increased his holdings. When he went on his cattle-buying trips to Chicago, wearing his overalls as usual, he was sometimes rebuffed by hotel clerks and salesmen. At such times he would give the name of his banker, and a quick phone call established his financial stability. He was known as a hard-working, hard-bargaining slave driver. But now that he's turned out to be a millionaire, the other side of the picture is beginning to emerge. It seems Herman set up many a farmer on his holdings in Maryland, Virginia, West Virginia, and Pennsylvania, and never foreclosed on any of them even in the Depression, when they couldn't keep up their payments.

Once, when he paid $2,000 for a prize bull at a county fair, the girl who had raised the bull started crying, so Herman let her keep the bull *and* the money.

Herman lived on a 156-acre farm near Gaithersburg, Maryland. His best friends were his housekeeper, Bessie Mills, and his cousin, Robert Stiles. Until 1963 Miss Mills and Rabbitt lived in a little frame house without a bathroom. When Miss Mills finally rebelled against this primitive way of life and left his employ to live with relatives, Herman built a nice new brick house with a bathroom to lure her back. She was lured. And eventually she helped Herman bury his horde of bank notes, silver, and old coins in some milk cans and an oil drum. In a deposition filed in circuit court, Ms. Mills, now in her seventies, said the new house was part of a written agreement she made with Rabbitt when he asked her to return. The house was to be hers until her death, and the buried money was to become hers upon her employer's death, she said. That written agreement has not been made public yet. Ms. Mills also says the amount buried was "in excess of $735,000."

In his will, dated August 8, 1966, Herman Rabbitt bequeathed Bessie Mills "all of my household goods and furnishings, equipment, machinery, livestock, and all other tangible personal property located at or about my home at Locust Grove Farm, near Gaithersburg, Md." But by the time of his death, Rabbitt had sold the farm, being allowed to live on there as a tenant.

Rabbitt's will bequeathed each of the living children of his half brother, Joseph C. Rabbitt, the sum of $1,000.

Note this bequest in particular: "I give, devise and bequeath unto Charles H. Rau of 2857 Montrcl Avenue, Eau Gallie, Florida, the sum of $1,000." More anon.

Finally, the will of 1966 bequeathed "all the rest and residue of my Estate whether real, personal or mixed of whatsoever kind or character, however acquired wheresoever situate absolutely and in fee simple unto Robert E. Stiles [his cousin] of Shady Grove Road, Rockville, Md."

In a codicil to his will, dated January 29, 1968, Rabbitt

stated: "To amend my Last Will and Testament dated Aug. 8, 1966, I give, devise and bequeath unto my housekeeper Bessie V. Mills, the sum of $2,000 in place and instead of the items of personal property heretofore mentioned in my said will."

Bessie is suing the estate, claiming the buried treasure. Stiles, who received the bulk of the estate, is keeping quiet and holding his breath. And guess who is suing for the whole estate? It's the aforementioned Charles H. Rau, now a resident of Long Island. Rau claims he is the illegitimate son and rightful heir of Herman Rabbitt. His court deposition says he is also known as Charles Herman Rabbitt, Jr., and that at the time he drew the will Rabbitt was "suffering from an insane delusion about the value of his estate and the relationship to and love and affection which he should experience toward Rau."

Washington officials say their records show a birth certificate for a Charles Herman Rabbitt, Jr., born at 1:40 A.M., August 26, 1937, at Georgetown University Hospital. The certificate lists the father of the child as Charles Herman Rabbitt, of Gaithersburg; occupation, cattle dealer. The mother is listed by her maiden name only as Louisa Rau; occupation, housewife. The "legitimate" box on the certificate is checked.

Maryland law does not automatically grant inheritance rights to illegitimate children, and even if Rau could establish that Rabbitt was his father, it would not mean he would automatically inherit any of the estate, according to news stories.

Chapter 22

A Playboy's Will

The actual life of movie actor Errol Flynn was every bit as romantic and dashing as the swashbuckling roles he played in pictures. He was born in Tasmania, where his Irish father and mother were cruising on a marine biological study. He went to school in Paris, London, and Sydney, and reportedly ran away from all of the schools. He spent a few years in the South Seas in a wide variety of jobs, ranging from cook to newspaper correspondent to pearl diver to copra trader to fisherman. His introduction to acting came when his boat was chartered by two Americans making a movie of jungle headhunters in New Guinea. He looked so good in that footage he was given a role in a film that never appeared outside of Australia but that whetted his appetite to be a movie actor.

Flynn went to England to study acting, was seen by talent scouts in his first major role, and was signed for Hollywood. The picture that gave him stardom was *Captain Blood*, which picture set the pattern for his career in the movies. His adventurous spirit sent him to Cuba to campaign with rebel leader Fidel Castro, further proof that he liked to live his movie roles in reality. He really wanted to be a writer, but his two novels, *Beam End* and *The Showdown*, proved he was better as an actor.

His romantic adventures, both marital and extramarital, garnered reams of publicity for Flynn. He had three wives: French actress Lili Damita, by whom he had a son, Sean; Nora Eddington, by whom he had two daughters, Deirdre and Rory; and Patrice Wymore, by whom he had a daughter, Arnella. Before, during, and after these marriages he preferred

liaisons with very young girls, three of whom charged him
with rape. He was acquitted of all three charges. His last
tempestuous affair was with Beverly Aadland, which began
when she was a teen-ager and continued until his death in
1959. After Flynn's death Beverly sued his estate for
$5,000,000, charging that Flynn had introduced her to "an
immoral life of debauchery." Even though she substituted the
word "debauchery" for the word "seduction" in her suit, Beverly couldn't evade the fact that breach of promise and seduction actions were outlawed in 1935, and she lost the suit.

After Flynn's death, actor William Marshall wrote a book
called *The Deal*, which minimized Flynn's romantic adventures by pointing out his physical shortcomings and endow-
ments. The hero of the book was not called Flynn, but it was
a very thinly disguised characterization. Marshall thought
Flynn had foxed him in a deal, and this was his way of striking
back. Whatever the reason for writing it, *The Deal* was a
thoroughly absorbing book.

Flynn's son Sean grew up to follow his father's footsteps
in looks, acting, and adventure. A tall, extremely handsome,
and intelligent boy, Sean played in several movies. Then his
adventurous spirit sent him to cover the Vietnam War as a
photographer and correspondent. He disappeared in Cam-
bodia, and no word has ever been heard from him since.

Not surprisingly, the will of Errol Flynn got as much publicity as his live escapades. The figures regarding his estate
were as varied, in newspaper reports, as the stories on Flynn
had been during his lifetime. The first report said he left an
estate of $1,800,000 and that the estate's attorneys were seek-
ing to dispense with a bond pending an appeal from a $75,000
judgment against the estate, growing out of a loan made to
Flynn by the Morgan Guaranty Trust Company. The loan
was guaranteed by chain store heir Huntington Hartford in
connection with a film Hartford intended to produce starring
Flynn. Next came a story that the estate was hopelessly in-
solvent, with not nearly enough left to pay Uncle Sam for
income tax claims. The next report, in 1963, four years after

Flynn's death, was that one of the executors had appealed to the surrogate court to set aside two judgments totaling $93,000, which the Morgan Guaranty Trust Company was trying to collect. The executor at that time said the estate's total assets were $1,160,000 and the total claims against it were $1,300,000, with insufficient assets left to pay the trust company's claims. In the meantime, the estate was trying to recover $100,000 from Huntington Hartford for alleged breach of contract.

In his will, Flynn had stipulated that his ex-wife Nora Eddington Haymes was to receive $45,000 for the support of their two daughters, Deirdre and Rory, each of whom was also to receive $10,000. His son was to receive $5,000, his daughter Arnella was willed nothing, and his parents were to benefit from his property in the West Indies. Beverly Aadland received nothing in the will. The residue was to go to Flynn's widow Patrice. According to a 1966 story, a compromise was worked out between Patrice and the other Flynn heirs, and Patrice received the residue of the estate. One would think that would have ended it. But then along came a story in a London newspaper in 1969 saying a court ordered the trustees of Flynn's estate to pay a $230,408 debt he never honored when he was alive to—guess who—the Morgan Guaranty Trust Company of New York, money borrowed in 1957. The British administrators of his estate claimed the debt was barred by a limitations act, but the court ruled it was not, according to the story. As in so many will litigations, around and around it goes, and where it ends nobody knows.

Chapter 23
The Clergy

The wills of members of the clergy are seldom unusual or liti-
gated. Since most Catholic priests take a vow of poverty when
they become priests, they have little to will except their few
personal possessions. The will of Pope John XXIII contained
five pages of blessings and reiterations of his faith, but left
nothing material. He had arranged the disposition of such
personal items as his fountain pen to his brother, and one of
the two pectoral crosses he wore during his papacy to Richard
Cardinal Cushing of Boston. By tradition, the ring he wore
as Pope was smashed and disposed of. Yet the Pope enjoyed
more pomp, rich trappings, glory, and reverence, and was in
charge of more of the earth's treasures than any other man on
earth.

Such properties and funds as do accrue to Catholic religious
during their tenure are usually transmitted to their successors,
as Cardinal Cushing did in his will. Cardinal Cushing also
willed the books, vestments, and other appurtenances of his
office to the Propagation of the Faith of Boston, Inc., for distribution among poor priests and prelates in the mission fields.
The residue of his estate, of whatever nature, was willed to the
Roman Catholic Archbishop of Boston.

When a Catholic priest or nun does will something valuable
to anyone other than the Church, it causes quite a commotion. Thus the will of the Reverend Michael J. Kenely, pastor
of St. Martha's Church in the small town of Kennebunk, Maine,
leaving the residue of his estate, after certain other bequests,
to his housekeeper, Marion Casey, stirred up a brouhaha.
Besides being a very religious man, Reverend Kenely was

also an astute businessman. Having inherited a small amount
of money from his family many years back, he enjoyed studying the market and making investments in "blue chip" stocks,
such as Anaconda, Chase Manhattan Bank of New York, Commonwealth Edison, First National City Bank of both New
York and Boston, General Motors, RCA, and Standard Oil of
both New Jersey and Indiana, plus fifty other stocks of like
quality. In time he amassed a fortune of $1,200,000. He had
four savings accounts with balances of over $36,000, and his
four checking accounts contained over $70,000.

The will Reverend Kenely left when he died at the age of
seventy-three made headlines and was contested by a niece.
The will bequeathed $5,000 to St. Charles College of Catons-
ville, Maryland; $5,000 to Weston College, Weston, Massachu-
setts; $1,000 for the saying of masses for the repose of his soul;
and the residue of his estate of whatever nature, including
the proceeds of insurance policies, to Marion E. Casey, of
Portland, Maine. The First Portland Bank and Marion Casey
were named executor and executrix, respectively, of the estate
without bond.

A niece, Mrs. Oliver Jones of North Grafton, Massachusetts,
contested the will, which was made ten years prior to Reverend Kenely's death, on the ground that when he made the
will the priest was not of sound and disposing mind and memory and not capable of understanding the nature of the act
he was performing. The niece claimed "the instrument filed
and represented to be the will of the decedent, was executed
under fraud and undue influence by which the decedent's
own intentions were controlled and supplanted by those of
another person, the same being in this case the person named
as the principal beneficiary, Marion Casey." The case was decided in favor of Marion Casey.

The public administrator of New York undoubtedly numbers among his more interesting cases the disposition of the
property of a saint. Mother Francesca Cabrini, who died in
1917 and was canonized as a saint in 1937, left a will that

turned out to be a poser. The will, hand-written in 1894, was extremely simple. The spelling and underscoring are as they appeared: "I, Francis X. Cabrini hereafter shall name Clothilde Lombardi of Joseph the hereiss of all I possess at the time of my death, nothing excluse. This is my last will and I subscribe it in presence of the wittness." It was signed by a Lucy Martin and a Mary Callaghan, and was written before Mother Cabrini had mastered the English language.

There followed a memorandum describing the property as that certain lot, piece, or parcel of land situated and being in the Borough of Manhattan on the southerly side of Twentieth Street between Second and Third Avenues, the boundaries of which are more particularly described in a deed from Arthur Smith to Francesca Cabrini. That plot of land in New York designated on map of property in Washington Heights in 12th ward. Described in deed from Marshall Margaret Grund to Francesca Cabrini. The first parcel of land contained the Columbus Hospital and the second parcel a high school.

All went well until Clothilde Lombardi, also known as Mother Josephine Lombardi, passed away in 1934, having neglected to make a will. It became the problem of the public administrator of the County of New York as to what would become of the property that Clothilde Lombardi owned outright. The final decision was that the property belonged not to one person but to the Missionary Sisters of the Sacred Heart.

That decision would have pleased Mother Cabrini, who was the first to start an order of women missionaries, in Italy, which finally came to be known as the Missionaries of the Sacred Heart. Her missionary work began in America, of all places. Greatly perturbed by the wave of emigration from Europe to the United States, and fearful that with the lack of churches, priests, and doctors the poor Italian immigrants would be easy prey to Protestant proselytizing, she burned with a desire to go to the United States to help them keep their faith. Learning from Bishop Corrigon of New York that the wealthy wife of Count Palma di Cesola had just raised $5,000 to start an orphanage but needed nuns to staff it, Pope Leo XIII gave his permission to Mother Cabrini to take six of her nuns to go to the United States.

By the time the seasick, bedraggled little group of nuns arrived in New York, the bishop had had a falling out with the Italian countess over the location of the house for an orphanage. He turned the group over to the Irish Sisters of Charity, where they immediately set to work to gather orphans off the streets and teach them in the choir loft of the convent, which was inadequate for the growing numbers of children. Mother Cabrini appealed to the bishop, and he allowed the orphans to move to the house the countess had selected. The nuns took to begging alms in the streets to raise the money they needed for the orphans.

With a small windfall, Mother Cabrini began acquiring more land and housing for setting up more orphanages. Some of the property acquired was in West Park, and Mother paid the rent on two houses by begging in the streets. Then out of the blue the New York State Senate passed a resolution that the funds from the poorly administered Garibaldi Hospital was to be turned over to them. Doctors, Catholic and Protestant alike, offered their services for nothing and brought surgical instruments. This was the founding of the first of many "Columbus Hospitals" that would spring up in many parts of the country. By 1902, the hospital in New York was receiving and caring for well over a thousand patients a year. It would have been a joy to her to know that by 1973 the hospital would be going through a $55,000,000 expansion program.

Appropriately, the body of Mother Cabrini rests in the chapel of the Mother Cabrini High School in the Bronx, the only saint to be buried on American soil.

One would expect such spectacular religious drum-beaters as Billy Sunday and Aimee Semple McPherson to leave rather large estates, considering how many grateful converts they snared; but they didn't. When Billy Sunday died in 1935 at the age of seventy-two, he left his estate valued at $50,000 to his wife, "Ma" Sunday. "Ma" declared as preposterous the stories of the enormous amount of wealth amassed by her husband. She did reveal, however, that several years before his death, her husband had provided trust funds for herself, two surviving children, and for the children of a son and daughter who died in 1933. At no time would she discuss the amount of the trusts.

Aimee Semple McPherson led a most active and hectic personal life that included three husbands and a false claim to have been kidnaped, besides organizing the Four Square Gospel and attracting a huge following as an evangelist. She died in 1932 of what a coroner's report stated was the result of an "accidental overdose of sleeping tablets." Her personal property was valued at less than $10,000, and her will directed that it was to be distributed to "blood relatives." Her son, the Reverend Rolf McPherson, succeeded her as head of the denomination. Aimee's mother stated that all donations and proceeds in the temple had gone back for maintenance and development.

The life of Mary Baker Eddy, founder of Christian Science, was fraught with calamities, almost constant illness, difficulties in founding her science of healing through faith, and countless vicious smears against her name, including a rumor that she was a morphine addict. However, she weathered it all and died at the age of eighty-nine, remaining active to the day of her death. Twenty-two years after her death she was named in a nationwide poll as the American woman who had made the most valuable contribution to American progress in the past hundred years.

When Mrs. Eddy founded the Mother Church-First Church of Christ, Scientist, in Boston, Massachusetts, contributions poured in. Then she started *The Christian Science Monitor*, another source of revenue. She bought a home called "Pleasant View" in Concord, New Hampshire, and the disposition of that home seemed to be her main concern when writing her will. In her original will she gave the right to occupy "Pleasant View" as a residence to Calvin Frye and Joseph

Mann. In a later codicil she revoked that stipulation, and bequeathed the right to occupy the house to Irving C. Tomlinson and his sister Mary Tomlinson. In a second codicil dated three years later, Mrs. Eddy directed her executor to sell "Pleasant View" within three months and pay the proceeds of the sale over to the directors of the First Church of Christ, Scientist, in Boston, to be used for such purposes as the directors might determine. Mrs. Eddy made numerous smallish bequests to relatives and friends, the largest sum, $20,000, going to one of her coworkers, Calvin Frye, who was also to be provided with a suitable home at Mrs. Eddy's house in Boston. The church she had founded was closest to her heart when Mrs. Eddy made out her will. She bequeathed the Mother Church-First Church of Christ, Scientist, in Boston the sum of $50,000, and to the Christian Science Board of Directors of the Mother Church-First Church of Christ, Scientist, she bequeathed the sum of $100,000, in trust for the following purposes: "for providing free instruction for the indigent, well educated, worthy Christian Scientists at the Massachusetts Metaphysical College and to aid them thereafter until they can maintain themselves in some department of Christian Science." In a codicil, Mrs. Eddy gave the Second Church of Christ, Scientist, in New York City, a sum not exceeding $175,000 "sufficient to pay the indebtedness which may exist at the time of my decease."

The will was contested by her next of kin both in Suffolk County, Massachusetts, and in New Hampshire, but in both cases the decision was against the contestants, and the will stood as written.

Ralph Sockman, pastor of Christ Church, United Methodist, on Park Avenue in New York City for nearly forty-five years and a leading figure on the radio with his stirring, folksy sermons every Sunday, died a wealthy man. His estate was valued at $546,984.59, before taxes. Apparently he thought his church was rich enough to shift for itself, as he left everything to his wife, daughter, and grandchildren. In a codicil to the will he gave the Welthy Fisher Fund the sum of $5,000.

Rabbi Stephen Wise was for over half a century America's

foremost rabbi and Judaism's proudest champion. He was also the most controversial. He founded the Free Synagogue on the principle that it would minister to the needs of the community as well as the religious needs of its members. It would also give him a pulpit to speak from, as freely as he willed. And he did speak freely about both politics and religion. Just as he made the transition from conservative Judaism to reform, so did he make the transition from being a Republican to being a Democrat, thus becoming quite a political power. He was a strong advocate of the rights of labor to have decent wages and working conditions, and made many speeches on the subject. He worked for the establishment of the State of Israel, and lived to see his dream come true, but never got to set foot in Israel.

While Rabbi Wise was a militant man as far as injustices were concerned, in other ways he was kind and loving. There was no one too poor or too lowly who needed his aid or advice that he didn't take the time or the money to give it. When he died, his estate after debts amounted to only $50,000. A total of $2,000 of it went to the American Jewish Congress, $1,000 each went to the Free Synagogue and the American Friends of Hebrew University, and he bequeathed $500 to the National Association for the Advancement of Colored People. The rest went to his children, James Waterman Wise and Domestic Relations Justice Justine Wise Polier, and to his grandchildren.

Chapter 24

Search for a Son

Mabel Seymour Greer kept her secret from her husband Louis all through the nearly forty years they were married. However, she couldn't resist telling her maid, her chauffeur, several friends, and eventually, just before her death, her lawyer, that she had borne an illegitimate son when she was in her teens. She also named the father of the son, Dr. Willard B. Segur of Ware, Massachusetts, who was a premed student at the time of their affair. She believed Dr. Segur had adopted the boy, named Harold, and had left the boy well off on his death seven years earlier. Therefore, in her will, Mabel Greer left her fortune to Harvard University, her late husband's alma mater and beneficiary under his own will. Her lawyer disclosed the facts regarding Mrs. Greer's illegitimate child in a statement that accompanied the filing of her will. Shortly thereafter, the adopted son of Dr. Segur brought suit to upset Mrs. Greer's will and claim inheritance of her fortune. Thus started a weird court case that titillated newspaper readers in the late forties and inspired a book by Judge David Peck called *The Greer Case*, which later inspired a television special.

The executor of the estate conceded that Mrs. Greer had borne a son by Dr. Segur, but contested Harold Segur's claim that he was the son she bore. Harold Segur's lawyer, Lester Friedman, took the case on a contingency basis. Since a child has a legal right to half the estate of his mother, Segur only had to prove he was Mrs. Greer's son. If he could also prove Mrs. Greer was mentally incompetent to make a will, he might invalidate the will and inherit her whole estate.

Francis Wells was the attorney for the estate. There was also a third lawyer involved in the case, Joseph Cox, counsel to the public administrator of New York County. If the public administrator successfully challenges the validity of a will, either on the grounds of incompetence or undue influence, and there are no relatives to inherit, the state takes the property. Thus Cox and Wells were aligned against Segur and Friedman, but with different aims.

Mrs. Greer had always been very cagey about revealing her true age and background. Various witnesses had different stories to tell on both scores. Her background didn't particularly matter—even the very wealthy and social Mr. Greer had taken her at face value when he married her in 1908. The only salient points obtained from witnesses regarding her background were that she was supposed to have been born in England, was a chorus girl under another name in Philadelphia, and bore an illegitimate child in a boarding house in Boston at a very early age. That age was what mattered. Wells and Cox hoped to pin down that age, and prove she would have been too young to have given birth to sixty-year-old Harold Segur.

Annie Jackson, a maid who was with Mrs. Greer for nearly twenty-five years, testified that Mrs. Greer had told her she'd given birth to a son in a Boston boarding house, with Dr. Willard Segur present; had left the child in the boarding house; had never seen either the doctor or the child again; and had only heard of them when she read Dr. Segur's obituary in 1939. The obituary said Dr. Segur left a son and an adopted son named Harold. In reading the obituary to Annie, Mrs. Greer had remarked that the adopted boy must be her son. Wells and Cox seized upon this statement as a mere deduction by Mrs. Greer that the adopted boy of Dr. Segur was her son—not a known fact.

When questioned by Mrs. Greer's lawyer shortly after her death, Harold Segur had stated that he was born in the Lying-In Hospital in Boston in 1887, and that when he was adopted in 1901 by Dr. Segur and his wife Mary Theresa, his name was Harold A. Baker. Queried as to how the name Baker came into it, Segur said someone had told him that Mary Theresa O'Donnell Segur, his foster mother, had taken him at his birth for the purpose of blackmailing one Harold A. Baker, a Boston citizen, and inducing him to marry her. When called to the stand to testify, Segur said his earliest recollections were living with his foster mother Mary Theresa O'Donnell in a boarding house in Boston, then moving to Enfield, Massachusetts, when Mary Theresa married Dr. Segur in 1895. He recalled that his adoption papers stated he was born of unknown parentage at the Boston Lying-In Hospital and taken at birth by Mary Theresa O'Donnell Segur. When Dr. Segur and Mary Theresa were divorced in 1907, Harold remained with Dr. Segur and never saw his foster mother again. On the stand Harold Segur contradicted the statements he had made to Mrs. Greer's lawyer during that interview shortly after Mrs. Greer's death.

Wells and Cox made a motion to dismiss the claim on the ground that Segur had not made a sufficient showing to warrant continuing the case. Judge Delehanty denied that motion but granted an adjournment. Then the two lawyers had to find some way to prove that Harold Segur was not Mrs. Greer's child. Her actual age was to be the main objective of the quest. Mrs. Greer's stated age of twenty-seven on her marriage certificate in 1908 would have made it impossible for her to have been Harold's mother in 1887. They dug up old state hospital records on Mary Theresa Segur, in which she stated that two months after her marriage to Dr. Segur she had discovered that he was living with a woman named Seymour, in 1895. Then a child resulting from this affair would have been born around 1895, which would better fit Mrs. Greer's professed age and her description of a child born to her in her early teens.

The two lawyers' first stop was the Boston Lying-In Hospital, where they pored over old records for any showings of adoptions. They discovered the case of one Addie Weston, who was delivered of a baby boy in the hospital on February 25, 1887. The record showed that the baby was adopted on March 8, 1887 by Mrs. Mary O'Donnell. The witness to the adoption paper was Dr. L. A. Cliff. By then Dr. Cliff was dead, but his daughter verified his signature. The lawyers' next responsibility was to prove that Addie Weston was not a name taken by Mabel Seymour to disguise her identity. Who was Addie Weston?

By the time court reconvened, Wells and Cox had not yet learned about Addie Weston. Friedman hoped Addie Weston would turn out to be Mrs. Greer. During the proceedings two witnesses testified that they had been in a show called *Humpty Dumpty* in 1904 with Mrs. Greer, who then called herself Polly Ernest. They said Mrs. Greer had been between twenty-two and twenty-four years of age then, and that she couldn't possibly have been thirty at the time, as Ned Wayburn would never have a thirty-year-old woman in the chorus. These witnesses were the curtain raisers on the courtroom battle over Mrs. Greer's age. Her age as testified by various witnesses had a ten-year difference. If Mrs. Greer had been born as late as 1881, she could not have been the mother of Harold Segur, born in 1887. Wells dug up documents such as the application for a license to marry signed by Louis Greer and Mabel Seymour, the marriage certificate, a census record, and hospital records, in which the day of Mrs. Greer's birth varied from 1881 to 1884. If these documents were accepted, Mrs. Greer could not possibly be Harold Segur's mother.

There still remained the big question: Was there an Addie Weston? Wells and Cox decided to have the registries of wills in the counties of Massachusetts searched to see if the name of Addie Weston appeared anywhere. A further adjournment was granted for this search. The two young lawyers searching the registry records hit the jackpot when they found the will of William B. Weston of Duxbury, Massachusetts, who had died in 1905 and remembered all his children: George, Maria, Etta, Eunice, and *Addie*. They tracked down Addie's sister Etta, who gave them samples of Addie's writing. The writing was the same as the signature on the paper on which Addie signed over her son for adoption by Mary O'Donnell. Etta had not known of Addie's child. Addie's husband, Ernest Bailey, was contacted, and the revelation of Addie's illegitimate child came as a thunderbolt to him. Both Mrs. Greer and Addie Weston had kept their secret from their husbands for forty years.

The trial was concluded in August, with a record fifteen hundred pages of testimony. Surrogate Delehanty handed down his decision in December. Harold Segur had failed to establish that he was the son of Mabel Seymour Greer.

Thus ended the case, but not the story. Joseph Cox was still curious about the real son of Mabel Greer. When the trial ended he told his assistant to watch incoming death reports and keep an eye out for a Segur or a Seymour. One morning the assistant rushed into Cox's office in a high state of excitement. He'd discovered the death in Boston of a fifty-three-year-old man named Willard Seymour. Cox immediately rushed to Boston to see the public administrator. If the circus roustabout named Willard Seymour who died in the alcoholic ward of a Boston hospital was the son of Mabel Seymour, the right he had to contest her will and claim her estate accrued to the state of Massachusetts, of which he was a citizen. But the state of Massachusetts had to go to the surrogate's court of New York to assert its claim. Cox suggested a search for the birth record of Willard Seymour, and also of savings account and court records to ascertain if Mabel Seymour was in Boston at the time of his birth. He also suggested a search for some record of the child having been under the care of some state or private charity at some time.

The life of Willard Seymour turned out to have been a sad one. His mother had boarded him out, then disappeared from his life. Mrs. Mary Colson, with whom he was boarded, took him into her home, but the payments for his support stopped after two years. His mother had moved to Philadelphia, where she went under the name of Everett. She only sent fifteen dollars in support during the next three years. The boy was declared a neglected child and committed to the state Board of Charity. His behavior went from bad to worse, and he was expelled from a school at which he'd been given a chance for a higher education. After a jail sentence for petty theft he had numerous lowly odd jobs, including that of circus roustabout. He became sick and alcoholic and went to the hospital on July 30, 1947, the very day Harold Segur was ruled out as the heir to Mabel Greer's half a million dollars. He died in August, just one week after the trial ended.

A search of the records in Massachusetts had uncovered a savings account of Mabel Seymour in Boston in 1894, and a court paper dated September 19, 1894, charging Willard B. Segur with being the father of Mabel Seymour's child. These documents definitely placed Mabel in Boston at the time of the birth of Willard Seymour on May 27, 1894. The putative father had denied paternity of the child, and a settlement in bastardy proceedings had been made out of court. Cox had accumulated numerous other documents to prove that Willard Seymour was the son of Mabel Seymour.

The surrogate's court was reconvened on June 25, 1948, and the matter of Mabel Seymour Greer was once more called. This time Friedman and Wells were on the same side of the counsel table and Cox was on the other side, flanked by the Attorney General of Massachusetts and the public administrator from Boston. The issue was whether Willard Seymour was the son of Mabel Greer. If he was, the state of Massachusetts had the right in his name to contest Mrs. Greer's will on the ground that she was incompetent when she made the will. Then the state would be entitled to receive all her property.

Though discrepancies in Mrs. Greer's age cropped up again during this hearing, the judge ruled that the person who died at Boston City Hospital on August 19, 1947, under the name of Willard Seymour was in truth the son of Mrs. Greer. In the end the Commonwealth of Massachusetts divided the estate with Harvard, to whom Mrs. Greer had willed it in the first place.

Chapter 25

The Last Will and Testament
of an Extremely Distinguished Dog

Many a dog has been the beneficiary of a will, but only one dog that we know of in the world left a will, with the help of his master. His master was Eugene O'Neill, whose article with the above title was first printed in 1958 and reprinted in 1959 by Yale University Press. Here is "Blemie's" will.

I, Silverdene Emblem O'Neill (familiarly known to my family, friends and acquaintances as Blemie), because the burden of my years and infirmities is heavy upon me, and I realize the end of my life is near, do hereby bury my last will and testament in the mind of my Master. He will not know it is there until after I am dead. Then, remembering me in his loneliness, he will suddenly know of this treatment, and I ask him then to inscribe it as a memorial to me.

I have little in the way of material things to leave. Dogs are wiser than men. They do not set great store upon things. They do not waste their days hoarding property. They do not ruin their sleep worrying about how to keep the objects they have not. There is nothing of value I have to bequeath except my love and my faith. These I leave to all those who have loved me, to my Master and Mistress, who I know will mourn me most, to Freeman who has been so good to me, to Cyn and Roy and Willie and Naomi and—

But if I should list all those who have loved me it would force my Master to write a book. Perhaps it is vain of me to boast when I am so near death, which returns all beasts and vanities to dust, but I have always been an extremely lovable dog.

I ask my Master and Mistress to remember me always, but not to grieve for me too long. In my life I have tried to be a comfort to them in time of sorrow, and a reason for added joy in their happiness. It is painful for me to think that even in death I should cause them pain. Let them remember that while no dog has ever had a happier life (and this I owe to their love and care for me), now that I have grown blind and deaf and lame, and even my sense of smell fails me so that a rabbit could be right under my nose and I might not know, my pride has sunk to a sick, bewildered humiliation. I feel life is taunting me with having over-lingered my welcome. It is time I said goodbye, before I become too sick a burden on myself and on those who love me. It will be sorrow to leave them, but not a sorrow to die. Dogs do not fear death as men do. We accept it as part of life, not as something alien and terrible which destroys life. What may come after death, who knows? I would like to believe with those of my fellow Dalmatians who are devout Mohammedans, that there is a Paradise where one is always young and full-bladdered; where all the day one dillies and dallies with an amorous multitude of houris, beautifully spotted; where jack rabbits that run fast but not too fast (like the houris) are as the sands of the desert; where each blissful hour is mealtime; where in long evenings there are a million fireplaces with logs forever burning, and one curls oneself up and blinks into the flames and nods and dreams, remembering the old brave days on earth, and the love of one's Master and Mistress.

I am afraid this is too much for even such a dog as I am to expect. But peace, at least, is certain. Peace and long rest for weary old heart and head and limbs, and eternal sleep in the earth I have loved so well. Perhaps, after all, this is best.

One last request I earnestly make. I have heard my Mistress say, "When Blemie dies we must never have another dog. I love him so much I could never love another one." Now I would ask her, for love of me, to have another. It would be a poor tribute to my memory never to have a dog again. What I would like to feel is that, having once had me in the family, now she cannot live without a dog! I have never had a narrow jealous spirit. I have always held that most dogs are good (and one cat, the black one I have permitted to share the living room rug during the evenings, whose affection I have tolerated in a kindly spirit, and in rare sentimental moods, even reciprocated a trifle). Some dogs, of course, are better than others. Dalmatians, naturally, as everyone knows, are best. So I suggest a Dalmatian as my successor. He can hardly be as well bred or as well mannered or as distinguished and handsome as I was in my prime. My Master and Mistress must not ask the impossible. But he will do his best, I am sure, and even his inevitable defects will help by comparison to keep my memory green. To him I bequeath my collar and leash and my overcoat and raincoat, made to order in 1929 at Hermès in Paris. He can never wear them with the distinction I did, walking around the Place Vendôme, or later along Park Avenue, all eyes fixed on me in admiration; but again I am sure he will do his utmost not to appear a mere gauche provincial dog. Here on the ranch, he may prove himself quite worthy of comparison, in some respects. He will, I presume, come closer to jack rabbits than I have been able to in recent years. And, for all his faults, I hereby

wish him the happiness I know will be his in my old
home.

One last word of farewell, Dear Master and Mistress. Whenever you visit my grave, say to yourselves
with regret but also with happiness in your hearts at
the remembrance of my long happy life with you:
"Here lies one who loved us and whom we loved."
No matter how deep my sleep I shall hear you, and
not all the power of death can keep my spirit from
wagging a grateful tail.

Tao House, *December 17th, 1940.*

This sentimental epitaph to his dog by the great playwright Eugene O'Neill as a comfort to his wife Carlotta Mon-
terey O'Neill just before the dog died of old age, was first
printed (one hundred copies) for private distribution, and
later republished in full in *Look* magazine.

A torn, partly burned document in an equally defaced enve-
lope was delivered to the register of wills in Washington, D.C.,
on August 25, 1895. It had been posted the previous day at
6:00 P.M. in a letterbox in the northwest section of the city.
The assistant register of wills was mildly interested in the appearance of the letter, because an effort had been made both
to tear and to burn it. The letter was apparently a will, but the
reader paid little attention until he got to the name of the testator, J. Holt. That one made the register sit up. J. Holt had
to be Joseph Holt, a former Postmaster General of the United
States and Secretary of War in the last days of the Buchanan
Administration, and later Judge Advocate in the trial of the
conspirators in the assassination of President Lincoln. The
names of the witnesses to the will made the register's eyes
pop. They were Gen. W. T. Sherman, Sherman's wife Ellen,
and Ulysses S. Grant. The will was dated February 7, 1873.
Holt had died at the age of eighty-seven on August 1, 1894.
Where had this will been all that time? Who posted it?

The will of Mr. Holt was in the process of administration,
as it was believed he had died intestate, leaving an estate of
close to $180,000. Both his wives had died, he had no children,
and his only other relatives were nieces and nephews living
in Washington, D.C., Indiana, and Kentucky. Two of his
nephews had searched his residence looking for a will, but
found none. They had filed a petition stating Holt had died
without a will and asking for the appointment of an administrator. A local bank had been named to function in that
capacity.

The register contacted the executor named in the will, one

Luke Devlin, who filed a petition in court for the admission to probate of what now appeared to be Holt's last will and testament. This move was immediately challenged by the nephews and nieces, since none of their names appeared as beneficiaries. The two women named as legatees, a Miss Hynes and a Miss Throckmorton (the deceased's godchild), obviously wanted the will probated, though both admitted they had not known of its existence. Devlin himself stated he had never seen the will before, even though he was named as executor in it. Elizabeth Hynes testified that she had corresponded with Holt for forty years and believed that both the body of the letter and the signature were in his handwriting.

The relatives contended the will was a forgery, as they knew Holt had violently disliked Miss Throckmorton's father, and therefore was unlikely to bequeath anything to the daughter of his enemy.

The big question at the hearing was whether the defaced letter was real or a forgery. All three of the witnesses had died. Were their signatures valid? Senator John Sherman of Ohio testified as to the validity of the signature of his brother, the general. Col. Frederick D. Grant verified the signature of his father, President Grant, and P. Tecumseh Sherman attested to the validity of the signature of his mother, Mrs. Ellen Sherman. Others familiar with Holt's handwriting testified as to its validity. However, the jury decided the paper was not executed by Holt as his last will and testament. On appeal the judgment of the District Court was affirmed. It was then appealed to the Supreme Court of the United States. The main controversy was over the validity of the signatures of Sherman and Grant, with witnesses both pro and con. Finally the Supreme Court reversed the decisions of both courts and sent the case back for a new trial. But a new trial never took place, because the parties compromised their difficulties. No one knows why. Perhaps the most compelling motive for settlement was the testimony of Mrs. Grant, who was still living. She recalled that at a dinner she and President Grant had attended at the home of Mr. Holt, also attended by General and Mrs. Sherman, Mrs. Sherman had been summoned for five or ten minutes into a room where the gentlemen were smoking, and had come back looking as if she had some interesting news, which she failed to relay to Mrs. Grant. When Mrs. Grant read in the paper about the will that had been mailed in, she decided that that dinner party must have been the occasion for General and Mrs. Sherman and President Grant signing Mr. Holt's will.

So it was settled. But one question still remains: Who mailed the letter, and why was it mailed twenty-two years late? Here is the will:

> In the name of God Amen. I, J. Holt of the city of Washington, D.C. being of sound mind declare this to be my last will & Testament. I do hereby give devise and bequeath all of my property both personal and real to Lizzie Hynes—Cousin of my First wife & to Josephine Holt Throckmorton who is my Godchild & to their heirs forever. I do hereby direct that at my death all of my property be divided equally between them. Lizzie Hynes is to inherit hers at my death Josephine at the age of 21, her father Maj. Charles B. Throckmorton will hold her share in trust. I appoint Mr. Luke Devlin of the City of Washington, D.C. whose character I believe to be of the highest standard & who will I am certain carry out my wishes my executor. Signed and sealed by me in the presence of these witnesses in the city of Washington, D.C. February 7th 1873 J. Holt.

The witnesses' signatures are Ellen B. E. Sherman, U. S. Grant, and W. T. Sherman.

Ehrich Weiss, who changed his name to Harry Houdini and became the most famous magician in the world, gave his collection of books concerning the black arts and magic to the Library of Congress in Washington in his will, and bequeathed to his brother Theodore, professionally known as "Hardeen," all theatrical effects, new mysteries and illusions, and accompanying paraphernalia, to be kept secret during his life and destroyed upon his death. However, Houdini carried to the grave the secret tricks that set him apart from all other magicians: his secrets as an escape artist.

One of Houdini's tricks that could never be explained was that of being locked in a cell, completely nude, with the cell double locked and barren of furniture. The bet was that he would meet his captors for lunch within the hour. Sixteen minutes later he invited his captors to meet him for lunch, and thirty minutes later he met them, fully clothed. He explained his ability to have himself sealed in a coffin and stay submerged in water for several minutes longer than a famous Hindu fakir by saying, "It is merely a matter of control and a placid mind and nerves." At another time Houdini had himself immersed head first in a narrow tank scarcely wide enough to hold his body, shackled hand and foot. Apparently it was child's play for him to get out of that one.

Oddly enough, after all the harrowing escapades he had been through, Houdini's death was caused from a blow by a McGill University student during a stage act in which Houdini requested anyone from the audience to give him the hardest blow the person could administer to his abdomen. His appendix was ruptured. Because of this his life insurance policy, which had a double indemnity clause, paid his widow $50,000 instead of $25,000. Houdini also willed his widow, Wilhelmina, his dramatic library plus all household effects, trophies, jewelry, oil paintings, and the income from investments.

The Society of American Magicians was willed $1,000, and each of Houdini's two assistants received $500.

In a special clause directed to his brother Theodore, the issue of Theodore could only inherit from their father if they had been confirmed to Jewish laws and traditions. Houdini's father was a rabbi.

The first bequest of the will was $1,000 to Machpela Cemetery Association in New York City, to be accepted in lieu of taxes and charges for lots. The will specified that he be embalmed in the same manner as "his beloved mother" and that he be placed in a vault like his mother's.

The rabbits used in his act went to the children of friends.

Houdini was buried in the same solid bronze casket that had accompanied him during his travels and in which he had had himself immersed underwater for as long as seventy-eight minutes. This time there was no escape. However, his widow claimed that she had received through a spiritualistic medium a secret message she and her husband had agreed upon and that was kept locked in a vault to which only she held the key. The message was in part "believe Rosabelle."

> Sweet Rosabelle,
> I love you more than I can tell.
> Over me you cast a spell,
> I love you my sweet Rosabelle.

Not a very inspiring message, but fairly hard for a medium to dream up!

Whenever a famous, highly publicized personage dies, someone invariably comes forth with a claim against the estate. J. Edgar Hoover was no exception. He was in the public eye and ear from the moment he became head of the FBI in 1924 until his death, because of his position. His own private life was really private. He was happy with his home, his dogs, his constant companion Clyde Tolson, dining out in restaurants occasionally, but mostly staying at home. It was no surprise whatever that the bulk of his estate was willed to his good friend Tolson, who was also named his executor.

Hoover's personal property at the time of his death had a total estimated value of $326,500, in stocks and bonds, cash, insurance, civil service retirement, unpaid salary and leave, household effects, and jewelry. The will left $5,000 for the perpetual care of the burial plots of his father, mother, sister Marguerite, and himself in the Congressional Cemetery in Washington, D.C. Other stipulations included a bequest of $5,000 to Helen W. Gandy, $2,000 to James E. Crawford, $3,000 to Annie Fields, an equal distribution of all wearing apparel to James E. Crawford and W. Samuel Noisette, and specified personal jewelry to John Edgar Ruch and John Edgar Nichols. He also specified that Tolson was to keep or arrange a good home for his two dogs. In the event Tolson predeceased him, the bulk of the estate was bequeathed to the Boys Clubs of America, Inc., and the Damon Runyon Memorial Fund for Cancer Research, Inc., equally.

The first claimant was Carl E. Ott, acting in the capacity of a friend of Thomas W. Atkinson, a mentally incompetent person. He presented a claim against the $326,500 estate for

$450,000. It seems, according to Ott, that Hoover had directed that no investigation be made of a contention that the intimidation of homosexuals was involved in four incendiary fires at the Veterans Administration Hospital in North Little Rock, Arkansas, which destroyed recordings about the alleged intimidation. All of this happened many years ago; and, of course, nothing came of that claim.

In September of 1972 a letter was received by the register of wills in Washington from a woman we'll call Mrs. Hand, reading as follows: "Dear Sirs, will you please send me a copy of J. Edgar Hoover's will? I am his wife. We were married in Hall County, Georgia, in 1945. We have a son, named for my father."

Ms. Hand was sent a letter from the firm of Hogan and Hartson in Washington saying, "On behalf of the executor of the estate, your claim to be the surviving spouse of Mr. Hoover is denied. While we are certain that your claim is in error, if you have any proof of your alleged status, we ask that you please forward it."

When we queried the law firm as to the present status of Ms. Hand's claim, they said they had no comment to make. We then wrote Ms. Hand asking if she had proof of her claim. We received a letter from Ms. Hand's "guardian" saying, "I'm very sorry about all this, but Ms. Hand is a mental patient. Just at this time she's back in Georgia State Mental Hospital for treatment. For years when this sickness comes she starts writing letters and gets big things in her mind. Of course [what she wrote about Mr. Hoover] is all untrue."

Probably many a person has regretted writing the register of wills when they learned that not only the wills filed there but also all the correspondence connected therewith becomes public property, and can be perused by anyone who wishes to do so.

Chapter 29

Much Ado About Nothing

When J. P. Morgan's granddaughter Eleanor Satterlee married Milo Sargent Gibbs in 1929, wearing a fortune in jewels instead of the traditional strand of pearls, and the same Worth dress in which her mother had married her father, it made a big splash in all the society pages. When she died in 1951, willing most of her estate to her lawyer Sol Rosenblatt, with special provisions for her Park Avenue psychiatrist Richard Hoffman, it made waves in several courts, and in all the newspapers.

Very little was heard of Eleanor Satterlee Gibbs in between those two events, except that she divorced Gibbs for cruelty in 1948 and took back her maiden name, which hardly caused a ripple. What rocked the boat after Eleanor's death was the effort of her sister Mrs. Mabel S. Ingalls to break the will, which had cut her off without a dime. Mabel alleged fraud and undue influence on the part of Rosenblatt and Hoffman, and charged her sister was of such weak mind she didn't know what she was doing when she signed the will. In the end Mrs. Ingalls lost her battle to break the will; Sol Rosenblatt received the residue of Eleanor's estate, estimated at between $200,000 and $400,000; and Dr. Hoffman, with whom Eleanor had assertedly fallen in love, was bequeathed only an oil painting.

The court case went on for two years, and meantime the newspapers had a field day with stories about Eleanor's mental ability, her love for her married psychiatrist, Hoffman, and the puzzling question of why Eleanor bequeathed her estate to Rosenblatt rather than to Hoffman, after having told everyone she intended to leave it to Hoffman.

Mrs. Ingalls' affidavit stated Mrs. Satterlee met Dr. Hoffman "directly or indirectly" through Rosenblatt in 1948, the day after she left her husband, and Hoffman "immediately arranged for her to enter Park East Hospital as Eleanor was constantly under nervous tension and under the care of specialists in nervous matters."

Numerous witnesses were called to prove Mrs. Satterlee was love smitten with Dr. Hoffman. The superintendent of her estate in Bar Harbor, Maine, Charles Frederick Salisbury, testified that Mrs. Satterlee furnished a special bedroom, called The Inner Sanctum, in the Maine estate for Dr. Hoffman, wore to a local playhouse a Chinese pajama top that the doctor had given her as well as a ring and various other items of clothing belonging to Hoffman, and constantly spoke of her love for the doctor, who visited the Maine estate several times. Salisbury also indicated, as many other witnesses had done, that Eleanor had nothing of old J. P. Morgan's understanding of finances. Some witnesses had declared her incapable of counting up to five or comprehending the difference between a nickel and a quarter.

As further proof of Eleanor's mental incapacity as regards money, her former husband Milo Gibbs testified that she was given the task of copying the cost of grocery items into a household accounting book in order to make her feel she was actively participating in the household activity. In discussing this copying chore, Gibbs said, "She was not a moron. She was retarded."

Other friends testified that when Eleanor told them she was in love with Hoffman and intended to marry him, and they pointed out that he was already married, she said Rosenblatt "could arrange a divorce in half an hour."

One thing is certain: Eleanor kept both Rosenblatt and Hoffman busy. Being so childlike, she needed Rosenblatt's constant supervision in handling all financial matters, including petty disbursements. He also handled the last four of the twelve wills Eleanor executed at various stages. In a will executed May 7, 1948, two months after her divorce proceedings started, Eleanor left $50,000 to Mrs. Evelyn Chandler, a friend with whom she lived for some time, and $100,000 to Mrs. Chandler's son Norman S. Dike, Jr. In the next will, the following November 12, Mrs. Chandler was omitted, Dike was down to $50,000, and Rosenblatt was empowered to distribute the residuary estate to charity. Three months later a new will, dated February 15, 1949, dropped Dike, too, and set aside $150,000 for charity, to be distributed by Rosenblatt, with the balance given to Rosenblatt outright. Her twelfth will, dated November 3, 1950, left her former husband $50,000, left $60,000 to charity, $30,000 to friends in small bequests, and $50,000 to be used to establish Eleanor Morgan Satterlee music scholarships under the supervision of Rosenblatt. Rosenblatt, who was named executor, got the rest of the estate.

Besides caring for Eleanor in his role as a psychiatrist, Dr. Hoffman also "followed the case" of the cancer that finally killed her on April 11, 1951, and had to give clearance on any moves made, as she was "completely dependent on him."

Surrogate William T. Collins ended the case by ruling that he found no proof of external acts of fraud or undue influence on the part of Rosenblatt and Hoffman, and dismissed Mrs. Ingalls' objections to the will. Both men must have wondered if it was all worth it. Hoffman received only an oil painting. Rosenblatt won a moral victory, but not much else, as the costly court fights spread over two years "took away practically the whole $200,000 left him, and a final accounting might even put him in the red," according to sources close to the case.

In the end, it all sounded like much ado about nothing. Hoffman was certainly not the first psychiatrist to have a patient fall in love with him—or imagine she had. Rosenblatt was not the first lawyer to be willed money in gratitude for services rendered. The general feeling was that they deserved their bequests—and then some.

Chapter 30

Poor Little Rich Girl

Gloria Vanderbilt deCicco Stokowski Lumet Cooper was bedeviled by lawsuits of one kind or another from the age of ten on, so the expected court fight with her relatives over the will of her grandmother, Mrs. Laura Kilpatrick Morgan, who died in February 1956, was just one more chapter in the continuing saga.

Gloria is the great-great-granddaughter of railroad magnate Cornelius Vanderbilt. Her father, Reginald, a famous horseman, died when Gloria was eighteen months old, and Gloria was raised by an aunt, Mrs. Harry Payne Whitney. When little Gloria was ten, her aunt and her mother, Gloria Morgan Vanderbilt, went into court in one of New York's most sensational custody cases. The grandmother testified that Gloria, Sr., was an unfit mother, and the aunt won custody of little Gloria. For many years the two Glorias, mother and daughter, were estranged, but eventually became close again.

Gloria married Pat deCicco when she was seventeen. Her next husband was conductor Leopold Stokowski, over forty years her senior, by whom she had two sons. When she and Stokowski were divorced a bitter custody raged in court over the two little boys, and Gloria won that one. Her third husband was theatrical director Sidney Lumet. Her fourth and current husband is Wyatt Cooper, with whom she is extremely happy. In between all these marriages Gloria tried her hand at writing, acting, and painting. It is the painting that has brought her the most success, and she frequently gives exhibitions of her work. She is at the top of the heap, fashionwise and socially, and hopefully all the lawsuits are behind her.

Through her father's will, Gloria received $5,000,000 when she was twenty-one.

Another court fight seemed imminent when Gloria's grandmother, Mrs. Laura Kilpatrick Morgan died. Gloria's aunt, Lady Thelma Furness (whose biggest claim to fame was her romance with the Prince of Wales), stated that the first will of Mrs. Morgan submitted for probate on her death was not her final will. That first will named Gloria, the Guaranty Trust Company, and attorney Thomas B. Gilchrist as executors. Lady Furness claimed that a second will, dated June 16, 1955, "revoked and superceded all previous wills," and named Lady Furness and the Guaranty Trust Company as sole executors, thus cutting off Gloria from executrix's fees. The earlier will gave Gloria a major portion of her grandmother's large estate, and left $10,000 to Lady Furness; $10,000 to a son, Harry Hays Morgan; and $50,000 plus shares of stock to Gloria's mother, Mrs. Gloria Morgan Vanderbilt. When her aunt dropped this bombshell, Gloria politely said she would not contest a 1955 will if the document was properly executed. Obviously it *was* properly executed, as the 1955 will was upheld and Lady Furness was named executrix rather than Gloria. However, losing the executrix's fees couldn't have been much of a blow to Gloria, as in that 1955 will she received $100,000; her mother received $80,000; and Gloria's two sons, Leopold and Christopher Stokowski, received the large residue of the estate.

Gloria wasn't the first Vanderbilt to be involved in a court fight. The precedent started with her great-great-grandfather's will and the litigation that followed. The Reverend Webb Garrison recounted that story in an article for the *National Enquirer*.

In the late nineteenth century a two-year court battle raged over the estate of Cornelius Vanderbilt (nicknamed "Commodore"), whose fortune was founded on steamship and railroad lines—the fortune was estimated at over $100,000,000 at the time of his death. The question at issue was whether or not Vanderbilt was insane at the time he drew his will. The basis for the belief in his alleged insanity was the fact that Vanderbilt believed in messages from the dead and in supernatural visions. A variety of mediums and spiritualists testified that Vanderbilt had indeed relied on the spirit world to deal with disturbing visions, and a medium confirmed that she had put the eighty-three-year-old Vanderbilt in touch with his dead wife Sophie. The widow of another spiritualist testified that the commodore's son William had paid her husband to give the sick old man a phony message from Sophie requesting him to will everything to William. Despite all this, the judge ruled that such belief in spiritualism did not in itself establish proof of insanity. Claimants Cornelius Jeremiah and his two sisters did not protest or appeal the decision, allegedly because they had already settled out of court.

Commodore Vanderbilt left the bulk of his estate to his son William. He also left $500,000 and property to his second wife, and $250,000 each to five of his eight daughters. To three other daughters and another son, Cornelius Jeremiah, who had been out of favor with his father for a long time, he left only the interest from trust funds. It was Cornelius Jeremiah and two of the sisters who rushed to court to contest the will.

Chapter 31

A Church Benefits from an
Amateur Hour

Major Edward Bowes was best known, probably, for his "Amateur Hour," which was a network fixture and voted America's most popular radio program in 1935. Before that his "Major Bowes' Capitol Family" had been the oldest continuous program on the air. But these shows were only two facets of Major Bowes' colorful career.

According to the Associated Press obituary on him, Bowes, who died in 1946 just before his seventy-second birthday, was at one time or another honorary mayor of sixty-seven cities, honorary fire chief of fifty-seven, and honorary member of thirty-five chambers of commerce, five boards of trade, and seventy-five police departments. He was also honorary governor, brigadier general, and lieutenant colonel in three states besides his official "major" from the Army Reserve.

Born in San Francisco, Bowes' first job after graduating from grammar school was as a guide at a schoolteachers' convention. An expert at Spencerian penmanship, he wrote calling cards for the teachers in Spencerian flourishes at twenty-five cents a dozen. His next job was as office boy for a real estate firm at three dollars a week. In a few years he started acquiring real estate for himself, and eventually owned good portions of San Francisco's business district. The earthquake of 1906 wiped out his real estate holdings. When he started to rebuild, he correctly guessed where the new business district would be and more than recouped his fortune.

Bowes then moved east, building theaters in New York and Boston, producing plays, and ending up as managing director of the Capitol Theatre in New York, which he made a great success. His principal financial connection, aside from Edward Bowes, Inc., was a vice presidency of Metro-Goldwyn-Mayer. His avocations included auto racing, boxing, yacht racing, raising horses, playing bridge, and waging a continuing battle against vice in all forms. He also accumulated one of the finest art collections in the country.

Francis Cardinal Spellman was one of his close friends, and administered the final rites. Just a month after Bowes' death, it was announced at Mass at St. Patrick's Cathedral that the church was to receive $2,400,000 from Bowes' estate, to be disbursed at the discretion of the cardinal for the beautification of the cathedral or for the use of such charitable institutions as he might select. The cardinal immediately set aside $100,000 of the legacy to go toward payment for the restoration and renovation of the cathedral. In addition to this bequest, Bowes' will gave legacies to twenty-six relatives and friends ranging from $10,000 to $50,000 and bequests of $500 to $10,000 to sixty-one specified charity organizations.

When he died, Major Bowes had an estate estimated at $3,641,112; 43 savings accounts, 5 checking accounts; $6,993 worth of liquor; $215,000 in jewels; and $30,000 cash in a safe deposit box at the Waldorf-Astoria. His wife had predeceased him, and they had no children.

Chapter 32

A Politician's Will

Paul Powell, the Illinois Secretary of State, was fond of saying: "There's only one thing worse than a defeated politician, and that's a broke one." For over forty years the colorful Powell was an undefeated politician.

Although his highest public salary was never more than $30,000 a year, his estate was estimated at nearly $3,000,000, some $800,000 of which turned up as cash stuffed into shoeboxes, briefcases, envelopes, and a bowling bag. The money, most of which was found in a two-room suite he maintained in Springfield, the state capital, took three bank tellers more than four hours to count.

Also found in the suite and an adjoining storeroom were 49 cases of whisky, 154 shirts, 14 transistor radios, and 2 cases of canned corn.

Apparently not satisfied with a mock explanation offered by a state official that Powell "must have saved the money when he was young," the Illinois Attorney General and the Illinois Bureau of Investigation have launched an investigation.

Powell's will, executed in 1969, revealed the source of some of his wealth, much of which came from horse-racing lobbyists. He left $15,000 and all his stock in Chicago Downs, Inc., to Margaret Hensey, a forty-nine-year-old divorcee, who was his $18,000-a-year personal secretary and close friend. He was also on the racing association's payroll as a $20,000-a-year "consultant." Powell owned 15,400 shares in the race track; much of these shares he purchased at 10 cents a share. Valued now at almost $4 a share, the stock, which was not available to the general public, is worth around $600,000.

Two envelopes containing $50,000 were found in his office.

Stock in Fox Valley Trotting Association went to a former secretary; in addition to the shares, worth $100,000, she received $10,000 in cash.

A grand jury exonerated him of charges growing from a probe into stock purchases in a harness racing corporation whose legislative interests he had championed.

The chief beneficiary of Powell's estate is the Johnson County Historical Society Museum, which received the Powell family home, to be used as a "museum for the citizens of Illinois." The residue estate, in trust, will provide income for its upkeep.

While the will remembered a number of friends, Powell was also careful not to forget his enemies. In a $10,000 trust established to buy poinsettias for the "shut-ins in Johnson County, their purchase from the Bellamy Floral Shop in Vienna is forbidden." Mr. Bellamy said the long-standing feud stems from a misunderstanding between the two dating from the 1930s when Powell was mayor of the small Illinois town.

In addition to his cash hoard and race-track holdings, the estate of the twice-widowed, childless Powell included over $400,000 of investments in small banks and insurance companies.

A $50,000 bequest was made in the will to the Southern University Foundation, to be used "for furtherance of the study of the science of politics and government."

The will also directed that a "proper marker" be placed at his grave, bearing a replica of the state seal, together with the inscription: "Here lies a life-long Democrat."

Chapter 33

The Eyeglasses That Paid Off

Harold Lloyd was the highest-paid actor of the 1920s. He left his thirty-two-room Beverly Hills mansion in California complete with a swimming pool, a nine-hole golf course, a hundred-foot waterfall, and a reproduction of Louis XIV garden of the Tuileries, in trust, as a museum for the study of the motion picture in America. Mr. Lloyd made nearly five hundred films, thereby earning more than $35,000,000.

The horn-rimmed eyeglasses, which he wore without the lenses, became his trademark. They were eventually insured by Lloyds of London for $25,000.

Under the terms of the will, the estate will be maintained "for the benefit of the public at large, specifically as an educational facility and museum for public viewing and scholarly research into the history of the motion picture in the United States." The trustees were given two years within which to raise a sufficient endowment for the maintenance of the property.

The bequest to qualify under section 501(c)(3) of the Internal Revenue Code but should the estate tax charitable deduction be denied, the gift will lapse.

Certain personal items were made available to be used in connection with the museum. These included all motion picture films owned by the actor, 1920 and 1922 Rolls-Royce automobiles, a 1927 Packard, all paintings of which he is the artist, books used by him in a stage set (known as the "Magic Memory Books"), his personal library, and his theatrical memorabilia and scrapbooks, including his "Oscar" and Eastman Awards.

The residuary estate was placed in trust and divided into

seven equal shares, with two going to Mr. Lloyd's son, two to his daughter, one to an adopted daughter, and two to a granddaughter. His wife died in 1969.

Mr. Lloyd requested that at all times there should be acting as executor and trustee a bank, a lawyer, and a businessman, preferably one with investment experience.

Chapter 34

The Bishop Estate of Hawaii

The will of Princess Bernice Pauahi Bishop, last of the Kamehamehas, might have had the most far-reaching effect, on real estate certainly, of any will in history. It tied up the choice properties in the Hawaiian Islands for all time. It also provided schooling for children of Hawaiian descent for all time. The original will was executed in October 1883, and the several pages of codicils were signed a year later, in 1884.

Princess Bernice Pauahi Bishop inherited about 378,500 acres of land some 16 months before her death in 1884, willed to her by her cousin Princess Ruth Keelikolani. When prior personal holdings were added, they brought the total to over 400,000 acres. Very shortly after acquiring the land, Princess Bernice executed the will, leaving all this land in a trust to establish and support the Kamehameha Schools. In addition, her surviving husband Charles R. Bishop deeded some 60,000 acres of his own to the estate 25 years before his death, to be handled in the same manner as his late wife's properties. The large acreage has been held almost intact by the trust, only 18,000 acres having been sold in the past 10 years.

In the 1883 will, Princess Bernice gave sums of $200 each to 7 namesakes and friends, and $500 each to 4 women friends. To H. R. H. Liliuokalani, wife of Governor John O. Dominis, she willed "all those tracts of land known as 'Ahapuaa of Lumahai' situated on the island of Kealai in South Kona Island of Hawaii, to hold for and during the term of her natural life; and after her decease to my trustees upon the trusts below expressed." (Those trusts "below expressed" were the crux of the will. And incidentally, these Hawaiian names are not hard to say—you simply pronounce every single letter.)

The will stipulated monthly payments and certain parcels of land to Kahakuakoi and Kealohapauole, to Mrs. Kapoli Kamakau, Kapaa and Auhea (all apparently servants), but in each case what was willed reverted to the trust for supporting the Kamehameha Schools upon the death of the legatees. To her husband, Charles R. Bishop, Princess Bernice willed all the various tracts and parcels of land situated upon the island of Molokai comprising the "Molokai Ranch" and all the livestock and personal property thereon; also all the real property, wherever situate, "inherited by me from my parents and also all of that devised to me by my aunt Akahi, except the two lands above devised to Queen Liliuokalani for her life; and also all of my lands at Waikiki, Oahu, situated makai of the government main road leading to Kapiolani Park." (in other words, Waikiki Beach). Here again this was only for the term of Bishop's natural life, and upon his decease the land went to the school trust.

Her Majesty Emma Kaleleonalani, Dowager Queen, was willed, "as a token of my good will," all the premises situated upon Emma Street in Honolulu, known as "Kaakopua." Upon Queen Emma's decease the land went into the trust.

Five thousand dollars was left to be spent by Princess Bernice's executors in repairs upon Kawaiahao Church building in Honolulu. Five thousand dollars was also to be spent by the executors for the benefit of the Kawaiahao Family School for Girls. Queen Emma was also bequeathed the fish pond in Kawaa, Honolulu, for her lifetime.

The really important and far-reaching stipulation in the will was the thirteenth item. It goes thus:

> I give, devise and bequeath all of the rest, residue and remainder of my estate real and personal, wherever situate, unto the trustees named below, their heirs and assigns forever, to hold upon the following trusts, namely: to erect and maintain in the Hawaiian Islands two schools, each for boarding and day scholars, one for boys and one for girls, to be known

as, and called the Kamehameha Schools. I direct my trustees to expend such amount as they may deem best, not to exceed however one-half of the fund which may come into their hands, in the purchase of suitable premises, the erection of school buildings, and in furnishing the same with the necessary and appropriate furniture and apparatus. I direct my trustees to invest the remainder of my estate in such manner as they may think best, and to expend the annual income in the maintenance of said schools; meaning thereby the salaries of teachers, the repairing of buildings and other incidental expenses; and to devote a portion of each year's income to the support and education of orphans, and others in indigent circumstances, giving the preference to Hawaiians of pure or part aboriginal blood; the proportion in which said annual income is to be divided among the various objects above mentioned to be determined solely by my said trustees they to have full discretion. I desire my trustees to provide first and chiefly a good education in the common English branches, and also instruction in morals and in such useful knowledge as may tend to make good and industrious men and women; and I desire instruction in the higher branches to be subsidiary to the foregoing objects. For the purposes aforesaid I grant unto my said trustees full power to lease or sell any portion of my real estate, and to reinvest the proceeds and the balance of my estate in real estate. I also give unto my said trustees full power to make all such rules and regulations as they may deem necessary for the government of said schools and to regulate the admission of pupils, and the same to alter, amend and publish upon a vote of a majority of said trustees. I also direct that my said trustees shall annually make a full and complete report of all receipts and expenditures, and of the condition of said schools to the Chief Justice of the

Supreme Court, or other highest judicial officer in this country; and shall also file before him annually an inventory of the property in their hands and how invested, and to publish the same in some newspaper published in said Honolulu; I also direct my said trustees to keep said school buildings insured in good Companies, and in case of loss to expend the amounts recovered in replacing or repairing said buildings. I also direct that the teachers of said schools shall forever be persons of the Protestant religion, but I do not intend that the choice should be restricted to persons of any particular sect of Protestants.

In the fourteenth item of the will, Princess Bernice appointed her husband Charles R. Bishop, Samuel M. Damon, Charles M. Hyde, Charles M. Cooke, and William O. Smith, all of Honolulu, to be her trustees and to carry into effect the trusts above specified, and said that at least three of the trustees must join in all transactions. She directed that the number of her trustees should be kept at five, and that vacancies should be filled by the choice of a majority of the Justices of the Supreme Court of Hawaii, the selection to be made from persons of the Protestant religion.

Charles R. Bishop and Samuel M. Damon were named executors of the will.

In the first 1884 codicil to the will, Princess Bernice willed to Queen Emma Kaleleonalani, instead of the Emma Street premises, all those parcels of land in Nuuanu Valley, Oahu, for her lifetime. In addition to the previous bequests to her husband, Charles R. Bishop, she also bequeathed him the land known as Waialae-nui, Waialae-iki and Maunalua, on Oahu, and all the premises in Honolulu known as the Ili of "Kaakopua" extending from Emma to Fort Street to hold for life. She bequeathed to Kuaiwa and Kaakaole, old retainers of her parents, the land occupied by them in upper Kapalama, called "Wailuaakio," to hold for their lifetimes, then to revert to the trust. Kaluna and Hoopii were willed those premises occupied by them in Kauluwela, Liliha Street, Honolulu, for their lifetimes, and likewise Naiapaakai and Loika Kahua were given the land they occupied in Kauluwela for their lifetimes. Money was left to Lola Kahailiopua Bush, Bernice Bernard, the Reverend Henry H. Parker, Mary Collins, Maggie Wynn, and two servants. Samuel M. Damon was willed all that tract of land known as the Ahupuaa of Moanalua on Oahu, as well as the fishery of Kaliawa. She willed to Kaiulani Cleghorn the parcel of land and spring attached at Waikiki-uka, Oahu, known as Kanewai, for her lifetime.

The sixteenth and seventeenth items of the first codicil made further provisions regarding the school trust:

> I hereby give the power to all of the beneficiaries named in my said will, and in this codicil, to whom I have given a life interest in any lands, to make good and valid leases of such lands for the term of ten years; which said leases shall hold good for the remainder of the several terms thereof after the decease of such devises; the rent however, after such decease, to be paid to my executors or trustees. . . . I give unto the trustees named in my will the most ample power to sell and dispose of any lands or other portion of my estate, and to exchange lands and otherwise dispose of them; and to purchase land and to take leases of land whenever they think it expedient and generally to make such investments as they consider best; but I direct that my said trustees shall not purchase land for said schools if any lands come into their possession under my will which in their opinion may be suitable for such purpose; and I further direct that my said trustees shall not sell any real estate, cattle ranches, or other property, but to continue and manage the same, unless in their opinion a sale may be necessary for the establishment or maintenance of said schools, or for the best interest of my estate. I further direct that neither my executors

nor trustees shall have any control or disposition of any of my personal property, it being my will that my husband Charles R. Bishop, shall have absolutely all of my personal property of every description. . . .

In the last codicil to the will, dated October 9, 1884, Princess Bernice increased her bequest to Queen Liliuokalani by also giving her all that tract of land situated in Honolulu known as "Kahala," together with the buildings thereon and fishing rights thereto for her lifetime, to revert to the trust on her death. (That is the stipulation that affects the residents in the most exclusive section of Honolulu.) This codicil also slightly changed the bequests to Kapaa and Auhea. The last codicil also enlarged on the important thirteenth item of the original will, to wit:

Of the two schools mentioned in the thirteenth article of my will, I direct the school for boys shall be well established and in efficient operation before any money is expended or anything is undertaken on account of the new school for girls. . . . I also direct that my said trustees shall have power to determine to what extent said school shall be industrial, mechanical or agricultural, and also to determine if tuition shall be charged in any case.

How does this will affect real estate in Hawaii? Here's how! It is impossible for anybody to *own* the land upon which they wish to build houses or hotels in all the best sections of the Hawaiian Islands (particularly Waikiki and the area where all the rich people live in Honolulu, known as Kahala). One must *lease* the land from the Bishop Estate for long terms, usually thirty years. You own the house you build there, but you don't own the land it is built on, and there is always the worry hanging over your head about how much higher the rent on the land will go when the lease is up.

Every good hotel in Honolulu is on Waikiki or Kahala, and all the best homes are in the Kahala area, which extends from Waikiki up to the Waialai Golf Course, and since they all come under the Bishop Estate, they all have to lease the land upon which the hotels and homes are built. A case in point is the famous old Royal Hawaiian Hotel, one of the oldest in Honolulu. During several lease periods the hotel only had to pay $15,000 a year for the land lease. Then suddenly when the last lease was up, the rent was jacked up to a reported $250,-000 a year. Originally the Royal Hawaiian was surrounded by acres of lovely gardens in the back and space on both sides. Now, in order to meet the cost of the new land lease, they've had to allow hotels to be built on either side and in the garden to help pay the rent on the land. The oldest hotel, the Moana, couldn't bear the brunt of the new rent and sold out to the Japanese, who now own 40 percent of the hotels in Honolulu as well as the Makaha Club, and are buying up more every day.

If one is able to find an attractive piece of land *not* owned by the Bishop Estate, you own it in what is called fee simple, which means you own the land too.

Thomas H. Hamilton, special adviser to the Kamehameha Schools/Bernice Pauahi Bishop Estate, was kind enough to supply a fact book regarding the Kamehameha Schools, parts of which follow: All the money realized from the perpetual charitable trust called the Kamehameha Schools/Bernice Pauahi Bishop Estate goes to support its educational program. The will did not specify that only Hawaiian or part-Hawaiian youth could be admitted to the schools. That became the policy of the trustees, based on the provision of the will that gives trustees full power to regulate admission of pupils and because several statements by Charles Bishop indicated this was Mrs. Bishop's desire.

The Kamehameha Schools/Bernice Pauahi Bishop Estate is exempt from paying federal income taxes because it is classified as an educational institution. Thus when the Schools/Estate decides to sell land, as they are allowed to do when such sale is in the best interests of the Schools/Estate or is necessary for the establishment or maintenance of the schools, they do not advertise for bids, as that would make the trust a land dealer and could result in a loss of tax-exempt status. They do have to pay real property taxes. In 1971–72 the real property bill was $4,648,528, of which $4,009,577 was recovered from lessees, leaving $638,951 to be paid by the Schools/Estate. Also excise taxes totaling $645,387 were paid that fiscal year. In 1971–72 the annual rents were $8,775,805, with an additional income of $666,968 from interest, dividends, and other sources.

The rental income on such a large estate is so relatively low because the granting of long-term residential leases causes a reduced rate of return over a period of years as the land value rises but lease rents do not, for they must be fixed for long periods; land being developed under development agreements produces a very low rate of return during the early years of the development because income lags several years behind the rise in land value resulting from the developer's capital investment; some leases were issued many years ago, when 3 percent was considered an acceptable rate of return on secure investments; in several agreements with developers executed more than ten years ago provision was made that for a fixed period of years some of the income goes to the developer because of his investment. However, estate income has grown considerably during the past twenty years. In 1945–50 the total annual income amounted to $1,472,114, and in 1971–72 it was $9,442,773. Expenses in 1971–72 were slightly over $3,112,000. The total operating budget for 1973–74 is about $8,200,000 of which more than $7,000,000 comes from the estate. The average commission of each of the five trustees is $58,508 a year. The retirement age of trustees has been set at seventy years.

Since 1928 about thirteen hundred acres have been made available for public use, either free or for a nominal consideration. Individual sales to home owners are severely inhibited— only large tracts can be sold, which requires a purchaser with large financial resources who is willing to take the risk that the individual leaseholders will then be willing to buy their lots.

Nine percent of the land in the state of Hawaii is owned by the Schools/Estate, but in Honolulu it is all prize property downtown, on Waikiki, in Kahala and Waialai. The percentage of the total land located on each island owned by the Schools/Estate is as follows: Oahu, 15.9 percent; Maui, 0.7 percent; Molokai, 1.3 percent; Hawaii, 78.9 percent; and Kauai, 3.2 percent. The island of Hawaii is the locale of the huge Parker ranch and the Rockefeller brothers' resort "Mauna Kea." Though most of the land is in the big island of Hawaii, it does not produce most of the income because of wasteland in gullies, land above the forest line, pasture land, and agricultural land having low productivity. The island of Oahu, where Honolulu is located, produces over 90 times the rent that the island of Hawaii does.

The Kamehameha Schools are located on a 422-acre site on Kapalama Heights in Honolulu. The trustees have stuck to their long-standing policy of giving preference to only Hawaiian or part-Hawaiian youngsters. The present practice is said to be to accept admission applications for the campus education program from any child whose parents or legal guardians are bona fide residents of the state of Hawaii, but the fact remains that right now no students who do not have some portion of Hawaiian ancestry are enrolled in Kamehameha's campus program, except for a few exchange students from the mainland. However, a number of different races are represented because of the racial mixtures in almost all of the students. The broad ethnic diversity of the student body is revealed in this table: 5 students are pure Hawaiian; 19 are seven-eighths Hawaiian; 69 are three-quarters Hawaiian; 180 are five-eighths Hawaiian; 344 are half Hawaiian; 490 are three-eighths Hawaiian; 730 are one-quarter Hawaiian; 660 are one-eighth Hawaiian; and 89 are one-sixteenth Hawaiian or less. The other races represented here are of Chinese, Japanese, Filipino, or Caucasian ancestry.

There are small assessments for tuition, fees, and meals, but those students unable to pay are helped through Kamehameha's Financial Aid Department, with grants made according to the various needs.

While would-be home and hotel owners are not ecstatic over Mrs. Bishop's will, several thousand students *are*. And her lands, which were appraised at $800,000 a few years after she wrote her will, now have a tax assessment of more than $360,500,000.

Chapter 35

The Will of an Insane Man— But Was He?

Charles Lounsberry, once a prominent member of the Chicago bar, later lost his mind, was committed to the Cook County Asylum at Dunning, and died there, penniless. He wrote a will so perfect in form and detail that no fault could be found in its legal phraseology. Read it, and decide whether he was rich or poor, sane or insane.

I, Charles Lounsberry, being of sound and disposing mind and memory, do hereby make and publish this, my last will and testament, in order, as justly as may be, to distribute my interest in the world among succeeding men.

That part of my interest, which is known in law and recognized in the sheep-bound volumes as my property, being inconsiderable and of no account, I make no disposition of in this, my will. My right to live, being but a life estate, is not at my disposal, but these things excepted, all else in the world I now proceed to devise and bequeath.

ITEM: I give to good fathers and mothers in trust for their children, all good little words of praise and encouragement, and all quaint pet names and endearments, and I charge said parents to use them justly, but generously, as the needs of their children shall require.

ITEM: I leave to children inclusively, but only for the term of their childhood, all and every, the flowers of the fields, and the blossoms of the woods, with the right to play among them freely according to the customs of children, warning them at the same time against thistles and thorns. And I devise to children the banks of the brooks and the golden sands beneath the waters thereof, and the odors of the willows that dip therein and the white clouds that float high over the giant trees. And I leave the children the long, long days to be merry in, in a thousand ways, and the night, and the moon, and the train of the Milky Way to wonder at, but subject, nevertheless, to the rights hereinafter given to lovers.

ITEM: I devise to boys jointly, all the useful, idle fields and commons where ball may be played; all pleasant waters where any may swim; all snowclad hills where one may coast; and all streams and ponds where one may fish, or where, when grim winter comes, one may skate, to have and to hold these same for the period of their boyhood. And all meadows, with the clover blossoms and butterflies thereof; the woods with their appurtenances, the squirrels and the birds and echoes and strange noises, and all distant places which may be visited, together with the adventures there found. And I give to said boys each his own place at the fireside at night, with all the pictures that may be seen in the burning wood, to enjoy without let or hindrance, and without any encumbrance of care.

ITEM: To lovers, I devise their imaginary world with whatever they may need, as the stars of the sky, the red roses by the wall, the bloom of the hawthorn, the sweet strains of music, and aught else they may desire to figure to each other the lastingness and beauty of their love.

ITEM: To young men, jointly, I devise and bequeath all boisterous, inspiring sports of rivalry, and I give to them the disdain of weakness and undaunted confidence in their own strength. Though they are rude, I leave to them the power to make lasting friendships, and of possessing companions, and to them exclusively, I give all merry songs and brave choruses to sing with lusty voices.

ITEM: And to those who are no longer children, or youths, or lovers, I leave memory, and I bequeath to them the volumes of the poems of Burns and Shakespeare and of other poems, if there be others, to the end that they may live the old days over again, freely and fully without title or diminution.

ITEM: To our loved ones with snowy crowns, I bequeath the happiness of old age, the love and gratitude of their children until they fall asleep.

This will was first published in *Harper's* in 1910, and has been cropping up here and there ever since. There have been rumors to the effect that it is a fictitious testament written by a living Chicago lawyer. Whether that is true or not, it is a beautiful composition and deserves republication.

Chapter 36

Foreigners' Wills That
Benefited Americans

The lives of a great many Americans have been enriched through the wills of three foreigners: Cecil Rhodes, British-born South African statesman, financier, and founder of the Rhodes scholarships at Oxford; James Smithson, English scientist and founder of the Smithsonian Institution at Washington, D.C.; and Alfred Nobel, Swedish chemist and engineer, who founded the Nobel prizes.

At the age of sixteen Rhodes left England and joined his brother Herbert in Natal, where they grew cotton. From there the brothers went on to the newly discovered diamond fields at Kimberley, where they had rapid success. Cecil returned to England to attend Oxford, where he matriculated in 1873, and finally, between many bouts with recurring illness, took his B.A. degree in 1881.

Cecil Rhodes wrote his first will in 1877, making the colonial secretary a trustee and leaving his yet unmade fortune to form a society to extend the British Empire throughout the world, to recover the United States, to inaugurate colonial representation in the imperial Parliament at Westminster, and to found a power strong enough to make wars impossible. These ideas, modified in his five later wills, remained the driving forces of his life. His last will was made in 1899.

Even during his Oxford career Rhodes had been making a fortune at the diamond mines. Besides the Kimberley mines, he accumulated other claims, including the De Beers Old Rush. He finally had control of all South African diamond production, 90 percent of the world total, and then went on to

form the powerful Gold Fields of South Africa Company.
Meanwhile, he started his political career which culminated
in his becoming Prime Minister of the Cape in 1890. He re-
signed this position in 1896 after the fiasco of a conspiracy to
overthrow the Transvaal government, of which he was the directing spirit. After that he went to Rhodesia (named for him),
where he was buried after his death in 1902.

In his will Rhodes provided for the maintenance at Oxford
University of men from specified areas overseas. The value of
each scholarship eventually rose to £900 a year, for two years
in the first instance, and for a third year should the trustees
so decide in individual cases. The will mentioned the objects
he had in mind in founding the scholarships:

> 1. COLONIAL. I consider that the education of
> young colonists at one of the universities in the
> United Kingdom is of great advantage to them for
> giving breadth to their views, for their instruction in
> life and manners, and for instilling into their minds
> the advantage to the colonies as well as to the United
> Kingdom of the retention of the unity of the empire.
> 2. UNITED STATES. I also desire to encourage and
> foster an appreciation of the advantages which I im-
> plicitly believe will result from the union of the
> English-speaking people throughout the world.

The principles on which Rhodes wanted his scholars to be
selected are defined as follows:

> My desire being that the students who shall be
> elected to the scholarships shall not be merely book-
> worms, I direct that in the election of a student to a
> scholarship regard shall be had to (1) his literary
> and scholastic attainments; (2) his fondness for and
> success in manly outdoor sports; (3) his qualities of
> manhood, truth, courage, devotion to duty, sympathy
> for and protection of the weak, kindliness, unselfish-

ness and fellowship; and (4) his exhibition during
school days of moral force of character and of instincts to lead and to take an interest in his school-
mates, for those latter attributes will be likely in after
life to guide him to esteem the performance of public
duties as his highest aim.

The nomination of scholars is in the hands of local committees, appointed by eight trustees. Candidates must be citizens of the country they are to represent for at least five years,
and be unmarried; and they must have passed their nineteenth
and not have passed their twenty-fifth birthday by October 1
of the year for which they are elected. Candidates are judged
on their records and after a personal interview with the elec-
tion committee. Except in certain exceptional cases, candidates
are obliged to have attended a recognized degree-granting college or university for two years at least.

There seems to be no ready explanation as to why James
Smithson, an English scientist, left his whole estate "to the
United States of America, to found at Washington, under the
name of the Smithsonian Institution, an establishment for the
increase and diffusion of knowledge among men." Smithson
had never been to the United States.

Born in 1765 of wealthy parents, the first duke of Northum-
berland, whose family name was Smithson and a mother who
was a lineal descendant of King Henry VII, Smithson was
educated at Pembroke College, Oxford, and majored in chemistry and mineralogy. He later became well-known for his work
in those fields, and the carbonite of zinc called smithsonite is
so named in his honor. Smithson never married, spent much
of his adult life on the Continent, where his friends were the
leading scientific experts of the time, and died in Genoa in
1829. In 1904 his remains were brought to the United States
and interred in the original Smithsonian building.

Smithson's estate was left to a nephew, Henry James Hungerford, with the stipulation that, should Hungerford die with-

out issue, or should his issue die intestate or under twenty-one, the whole estate would go for the founding of Smithsonian Institution. Hungerford died without issue in 1835.

There was much opposition in the United States to the acceptance of Smithson's bequest, but it was finally accepted, largely through the efforts of John Quincy Adams. The first payment arrived in 1838 in the form of gold sovereigns, which was recoined into U.S. money. It amounted to $508,318.45. After Hungerford's mother died in 1867, a further residuary legacy was received, bringing the fund up to $650,000. By savings of interest and other gifts, the fund was increased. After ten years of debate, Congress in 1846 accepted the trust and created by enactment an "establishment" called the Smithsonian Institution, consisting of the President and Vice President of the United States, the Chief Justice of the United States, and members of the Cabinet. The act named those to be on the board of regents, and also provided for a library and a museum to contain "objects of art and of foreign and curious research, and objects of natural history, etc." belonging to the United States. The Smithsonian was probably the first establishment in the United States to have a staff of full-time research scientists in a broad series of fields.

Alfred Nobel was born in Stockholm in 1833 and was mostly educated by tutors. During his later travels to complete his education as an engineer, he spent about a year in the United States. On his return to Sweden he studied explosives, especially nitroglycerine, and in 1867 was granted a British patent for his invention of dynamite. He invented more explosives and also a method of detonating them. From the manufacture of explosives and from the exploitation of the Baku oil fields, Nobel amassed a huge fortune. He never married, was lonely, and suffered ill health all of his life, which made him pessimistic and satirical; yet he retained a certain benevolence and belief in the future of humanity.

At his death in Italy, in 1896, Nobel left the bulk of his fortune in trust to establish five prizes in peace, physics, chemistry, physiology or medicine, and literature. It is commonly believed that it was Nobel's distress over the uses to which his invention of explosives could be put that he made one of the prizes a peace prize.

These annual prizes are awarded by four institutions, three Swedish and one Norwegian. Distribution was begun December 10, 1901, the fifth anniversary of Nobel's death, with the awards going "to those who, during the preceding year, shall have conferred the greatest benefit on mankind" in the five fields. Each award consists of a gold medal, a diploma bearing a citation, and a sum of money that depends on the income of the foundation and has ranged from about $30,000 to $50,000.

Prizes have been declined, and in some instances governments have forbidden their nationals to accept Nobel prizes. The scientific and medical prizes have proved to be the least controversial, while those for literature and peace have been the most exposed to critical differences. The peace prize has been most frequently reserved.

A prize is either given entirely to one person, divided equally between at most two works, or shared jointly by two or more persons. The prizes are open to all regardless of nationality, race, creed, or ideology, and can be awarded more than once to the same recipient.

The presentations of the prizes for physics, chemistry, physiology or medicine, and literature take place in Stockholm on December 10, the anniversary of Nobel's death. The peace prize is presented in Oslo on the same date. The winners usually receive their prizes in person. Each prize winner who comes to receive his or her prize may bring along his or her wife or husband and all children under twenty-one. Thus the ceremonial presentations are attended by numerous children as well as proud spouses.

Quite fey and unorthodox is the will of a lawyer named Samuel L. Phillips of Washington, D.C., whose will was filed in 1968. It's all in poetry, right up to the signing of the witnesses:

This writing shall my last Will and Testament be,
For verily there are no others from me,
And while I state that my mind is sound,
A different opinion could be found.
Though my worldly possessions are few,
For a lawyer to die intestate just wouldn't do.
So now I must publish and declare,
That this writing so stylishly bare,
Shall devise my belongings true.

As for my funeral and where I shall lay,
Let those who survive me do what they may.
My mortal remains can be given an autopsy,
Who knows, I may have suffered from dropsy,
For I have been treated for many an ill,
Was I getting the right pill?
And if my medical treatment was out of line,
May the A.M.A.er's have better luck next time.

As for my debts, just and unjust,
And to any creditor who did me trust,
I hereby direct my executor to tell
Them all kindly go to hell.
Then posthumously in court we will fight:
For litigation is a lawyer's delight.

Now that the preliminaries have been completed,
And the reader's sensibilities defeated,
Let us now get on with the work before us,
And bequeath and devise my worldly corpus.

To my parents who gave me their all,
And whose hopes for me did wax tall,
I give them all my love and affection,
As this will not aggravate their income tax situation.
And any personal belongings I leave behind me,
Let them dispose of speedily,
To any one that they may,
For they shall do this anyway.

To the following legatees, I hereby devise
Not a very grand prize,
But merely the sum of one hundred dollars a piece,
Which is really the very least,
For a lifetime of intimate friendship and association.
They are: Curtis Davis
            Katie Ingram,
            The Jewish Community Center
            And the Kesher Israel Congregation.
And only upon one condition shall there be,
That the above named shall survive me.

As for my legal practice, as it may be,
Let my executor take what he may,
For this may be his only fee,
For the labor of many a day,
And what he does not desire,
Let my associates aspire
To wind up the same,
And pocket any fees they may claim.

Finally, what shall I now do,
With what we call the residue,
For whoever gets this lowly lot,
Could possibly end up with the jackpot,

And this legatee we do not call mister,
For it is my flesh and blood sister.
Helen Phillips Barnestone is her name,
And while her children I do not name,
It is my desire as she sees fit,
That it be used for their benefit.

Now I nominate my estate's protector.
Robert H. Symmonds, Esquire, shall be my executor.
And it is my desire without a doubt,
That he shall serve without
Any type of bond or surety,
To bind his fidelity.

Now that my task is complete,
Let no malcontent defeat
This juristic pearl
That I leave behind me in this world.

We, the below named witnesses three,
Have seen this writing be
Signed, sealed, published and declared by
Samuel L. Phillips, who asks us to comply
With the stated requirements of the law,
At his request and in his presence they saw
Him to this writing sign his name,
Whereupon, as attesting witnesses, they did the same.

The will of Walter Malloy, Ohio Bell Telephone Company
assistant manager of Columbus, Ohio, also in poetry, combined
some sage advice along with his bequests:

PREAMBLE
My mind is sound, my heart beats true
And, realizing what I do,
I take my trusty pen in hand
So probate courts throughout the land
May, after I have passed away

And faced my God on Judgment Day,
Know my desires, and see to it
My will is carried out, to wit:
The home is in my good wife's name
And I request it stay the same,
But she may do as she sees fit,
'Tis my advice, get rid of it
And move into a cozy flat
To cut expense; that settles that.
Should I survive my loving spouse
Hold title to the land and house
I will that, when I've run my race
My boy and girl shall share the place,
Should either one desire to live
In the home place, then they must give
Unto the other what seems fair
To purchase outright their half share.
If I'm possessed of surplus cash
A strange thing though it may be,
I will my wife shall have it all
For bills or doctor's fee;
I give her title to all funds
In savings or in check
And ask that she pay all the debts
So I'll be square, by heck!

PERSONAL ESTATE

Now any other worldly goods
That I have laid away
Will turn up in the safety box,
And this is what I say,
My wife shall have the whole estate
As long as she may live
To spend, to hoard, to dissipate,
To share, to save, to give.
But when death's angel beckons her,
Whatever may remain

Shall go unto my children
In this manner I'll explain:
In equal parts to Betty, John,
Or should they not survive,
Apportion 'mongst their children
Who may yet remain alive.
Of course, there'll be other small trinkets
That naturally go to my boy,
There's my watch and my ring, in fact everything
He can have, that he'd likely enjoy.
I lack a memento for Betty,
I don't own a thing that she'd crave,
So I send from above just a heart-ful of love
To cherish from now to her grave.
The inventory won't be great
There isn't much to my estate
But who's that coming in the gate?
The life-insurance man!
Here comes the cash, oh happy day,
He'll foot the bills and go his way
But every month he'll have to pay,
That life insurance man!
Lo, many moons those checks will come
For quite a tidy little sum,
He's one good friend you must not shun,
The life insurance man!

William H. Benton crammed several careers into his lifetime: He was cofounder of the advertising agency of Benton & Bowles; he was a U. S. senator; he was a vice president of the University of Chicago; and he was owner of the Muzak Corporation and of Encyclopaedia Britannica, Inc.

After taking several millions out of the Muzak Corporation in dividends, he sold it in 1957 for $4,350,000. He is credited with introducing applause by studio audiences by holding up signs. While still at the University of Chicago, Benton purchased the Encyclopaedia Britannica in 1943 from Sears, Roebuck and Company (the Encyclopaedia had its start in England in 1771). He put up $100,000 in working capital and gave the school a beneficiary interest that benefited the university by $25,000,000 in twenty-five years.

When Benton died at the age of seventy-two, he left the bulk of his multimillion-dollar estate to the William Benton Foundation. He stated in his will that his sons and daughters and the foundation trustees would be urged to make a public offering in Encyclopaedia Britannica stock. "I hope that you will resist such pressure," he wrote. "Do not yield to the Wall Street son of the Pied Piper and do not be tempted by the hope of profit or power as a public corporation." He noted that few companies of the Encyclopaedia's size are privately held, and said "there is no comparable corporation with Britannica's significant interest and responsibilities in the world. Although the Britannica should continue to offer great financial rewards to its executives and owners, it should never be regarded as merely a source of money or power."

Inserted in the will at this point was a translated Hebrew prayer:

> "For I give you good doctrine; forsake not my teaching. It is a tree of life to them that grasp it and of them that uphold it, everyone is rendered happy. Its ways are ways of pleasantness and all its pasts are peace."

Benton's will urged that the foundation favor the University of Chicago with its grants, and further added that if Congress changes the tax-deduction laws so that the foundation bequests become taxable, the University of Chicago should receive the nondeductible portion.

Seemingly irked at the wordiness of lawyers, Benton put in a protest at all the "legal gobbledygook" used in writing a will. "The lack of training lawyers in the art of clear-cut English in college and law school must help explain why so many lawyers are continuously kept busy arguing over the language of their predecessors."

Benton's widow was left a twelve-acre estate in Connecticut with a request that it be turned over to the University of Bridgeport on her death as a home for the school's chancellor or president.

Chapter 39

A Ghost Settles an Estate

In Queen Anne's County, Maryland, in the year 1798 or 1799, the appearance and existence of a ghost was proved in circuit court to the satisfaction of all present, except perhaps Mrs. Mary Harris, who was relieved of some real estate as a result of the proceedings. The story is at the Maryland Historical Society in a pamphlet whose pages now are as fragile and flimsy as congealed ectoplasm. The booklet, published in Baltimore in 1808, is entitled *Authentic Account of the Appearance of a Ghost in Queen Anne's County, Md.*

Here is the story, as relayed to us by Thomas J. White, executive editor of the Baltimore *News American:*

One night in March (the year is not specified), a man named William Briggs was riding his horse near a cemetery. Suddenly the animal began neighing, pricking up its ears and looking over the fence where, to Briggs' astonishment, the ghost of his late friend Thomas Harris materialized.

The ghost was dressed in a sky-blue coat, and it stood and stared at Briggs for a few moments before vanishing.

Much upset, Briggs went home, but he did not tell anyone what he had seen because he did not think he would be believed.

On the following June 1 the ghost must have been extremely restless and in a bad mood, because it made Briggs' day miserable.

It appeared to him first in the afternoon, once again keeping its silence, but that night, when Briggs went to bed, he heard a loud groan. So did his wife, who got up to see what was making the noise. While she was out of the room Briggs felt a great weight on him, and then he got socked in the nose so hard his eyes were blackened.

Two months later the ghost of Thomas Harris appeared to Briggs once more, and this time spoke to Briggs and explained what was bothering him, or rather "it."

It seemed that Thomas Harris had expressed the wish in life that when he died his real estate was to be sold and the money given to his four illegitimate children, a distribution that had not taken place. The ghost told Briggs to go to Thomas's brother James Harris and ask him if he "did not remember the conversation which passed between them on the east side of the wheat stacks the day he was taken with his death sickness."

Briggs went to James Harris, who recalled the conversation and accepted Briggs' story of the ghost because he said no other person knew of the conversation. James admitted that Thomas had said at the time he wanted the children to be his beneficiaries and he told Briggs he would take care of the matter.

But then James Harris up and died before anything could be done and his widow, Mary, claimed she was sole beneficiary to all of the Harris property.

That's how the case got into court. The four children sued for their share. Legally, illegitimate children could not share in the estates of their parents, but the courts felt that if the appearance of the ghost could be proved, then Mary Harris would have to turn the money over to the youngsters.

Thus everything hinged on the testimony of William Briggs. He was known to be a man of good character, a brave soldier during the Revolutionary War, and he had no personal financial interest in the proceedings.

In vain, lawyers tried to break down his story, and in the end it was agreed that the ghost had really existed. It was a great victory for His Excellency Robert Wright—later governor of Maryland—who served as counsel for the plaintiffs.

It was also a victory for the children who, in due time, received the money.

Chapter 40

Stephen Decatur

Many wills are written in the throes of a fatal illness, when the testator knows death is imminent. Stephen Decatur could only surmise that death *might* be imminent when he hastily wrote and signed his will at breakfast with a group of friends, then went out to be killed in a duel with his challenger, Commodore James Barron, on March 22, 1820.

Only forty-one at the time, Commodore Decatur was one of the most romantic figures in American history and the darling of the nation. In 1805 he had displayed his valor in hand-to-hand combat with the pirates of Tripoli. He had captured the British ship *Macedonian* in the war of 1812. He had caused the Algerian corsairs to surrender in 1815. In 1816, at a banquet in his honor, he had uttered the historic toast: "Our country: In her intercourse with foreign nations may she always be right, but, right or wrong, our country."

He had only lived for a short time in a mansion designed by Benjamin Latrobe and built facing Lafayette Square (then called President's Square) at H Street and Jackson Place—a house that still stands. He was handsome, lived a rich life, had a dearly loved wife, Susan, and was the most distinguished resident of the capital next to his friend President Monroe.

The events that led to Decatur's death seemed pointless. Commodore James Barron had been court-martialed after his ship had been fired on in 1807 by the British and forced to strike her colors. Decatur was a member of the court that suspended Barron from the Navy for five years. The embittered Barron went abroad and sat out the War of 1812. When he returned in 1818 and sought reinstatement in the Navy,

Decatur opposed his restoration to duty, and brought up the
fact that Barron had not returned to help in the war. In 1819
Barron started a correspondence during which thirteen letters
were exchanged with Decatur. Decatur accepted the last letter
as a challenge.

On the appointed morning Decatur left Susan peacefully
sleeping and joined his second, Commodore William Bain-
bridge, and a friend, Purser Samuel Hambleton, at Beall's
Hotel. During breakfast he showed the will he'd hastily written out, and declared he had no desire to kill Barron.

After breakfast they proceeded to the Bladensburg dueling
grounds, which enjoyed comparative safety from the law because of the extra business the duels brought local liverymen
and undertakers.

During the preliminaries neither of the principals spoke a
word. They were handed their pistols by their seconds, took
their places, and on the count of "two" fired simultaneously.
Just before the countdown Barron said, "I hope, sir, that when
we meet in another world we shall be better friends than we
have been in this." Decatur replied, "I have never been your
enemy, sir." Barron was struck in the groin. The bullet that hit
Decatur went into his hip and through his abdomen. As he
fell, Decatur said, "I am mortally wounded, I think. I wish
I had fallen in the service of my country."

As they lay on the ground with the surgeons working over
them, Barron, thinking his own wound was fatal, proposed
they make friends before they died. Decatur repeated, "I
have never been your enemy. I freely forgive you my death,
though I cannot forgive those who have stimulated you
to seek my life."

Barron is supposed to have replied, "Would to God you had
said this much yesterday."

Decatur was taken home, where he lingered on twelve
hours in agony before dying, during which time he would not
let Susan see him, as he wanted to spare her the sight of his
suffering. The entire nation mourned his death.

Decatur's brief handwritten will goes like this:

I Stephen Decatur of the U. S. Navy, now residing in the city of Washington make this my last will & testament as follows—I give & devise to my beloved wife Susan Decatur & her heirs all my estate real personal & mixed wheresoever situated, & I appoint my friends Littleton Waller Tarewell of Norfolk, Robert G. Harper of Baltimore, & Geo. Bornford of this city of Washington together with Mrs. Decatur my wife to be executor of this my will.

In witness whereof I have hereto set my hand seal this twenty second of March one thousand eight hundred and twenty.

The style and lack of punctuation indicate the haste with which the will was written.

Most vengeful wills are written by the testators by hand, without benefit of a lawyer, and are probably written in the heat of anger rather than on the deathbed. It's that last chance to strike back, to tell off a wife or friend, to have the last laugh.

Most of the real names in these vengeful wills will be changed, for obvious reasons.

Jack Dare willed his wife thirty pieces of silver or thirty dimes, the sum not to exceed $3.00—"the sum Judas received when he betrayed Christ at the Last Supper. Maybe she can add to it and buy some decent bourbon."

In a will dated in 1965, Lynn Smith left handsome legacies to "his beloved wife Kay" and his beloved daughters. In a codicil dated just two years later, he seems to have changed his mind about his wife. The codicil reads: "Now in conclusion you should know this. My wife Kay has been most ungrateful, disrespectful, contemptible and uncooperative and will not deserve what she gets from me when I have left this earth. I give her full credit for the physical and mental suffering I have had to endure for so many years. Had it not been for the children's sake I would have gotten a divorce long ago. I could write a book—she probably will in an effort to counteract these sentiments. It's regretful that I will not be around for a rebuttal. Just a little spark of love, it costs so little and means so much!" This embittered man died just five months after that last codicil.

The will of August Wieneke, dated in 1924, indicates his high regard for his son Frederick, but he apparently didn't think too highly of his other children or relatives. Frederick inherited all the money. He bequeathed to his sons William and Henry one hen and five cents each. Each of his three daughters, Augusta, Amelia, and Minnie, was to receive one rooster and five cents. "Should I have no roosters or hens at the time of my death, then my son Frederick shall purchase them with some of the money that I may leave. Should there be any other legal heirs, they shall each receive thirty-nine cents."

A Maryland resident named Karl Hughes willed to his wife "every damned thing that I own that she wants with the following stipulations: that my dog Lobo who is of essentially the same temperament as I be allowed more freedom than I have been allowed . . . that my stepson be allowed to learn that it is good to stand on his own earth and look at the sky, to wonder about nature and the universe, and in general to retain curiosity as does a child or a scientist." The will continued, "to my mother I return all of the love and torment that she gave to me; to my father I give all of the appreciation for that which he did all of those years when he could have, perhaps, done more. I do want it understood however that I like him as he is." To various friends and relatives, Hughes bitterly bequeathed "all the misery and problems and disturbances that I have suffered." The last sentence read, "And to the rest of the world I bequeath, endow, donate, as much as I can, a freedom from the plagues and tribulations that I have seen."

A wealthy banker didn't have a kind thought of anyone in writing out his will. He wrote, "To my wife I leave her lover and the knowledge I wasn't the fool she thought I was. To my son I leave the pleasure of earning a living. For twenty-five years he thought the pleasure was mine, but he was mistaken. To my valet I leave the clothes he has been stealing from me regularly for ten years, also the fur coat he wore last winter while I was in Palm Beach. To my chauffeur I leave my cars. He has almost ruined them and I want him to have the satisfaction of finishing the job."

The most vindictive will of all was written by a resident of Munich, Germany. His will stipulated that the wake was to be held in an upper story of his house. When his relatives

gathered around the coffin, the floor collapsed and most of
the mourners were killed. It was later discovered that before
his death the man had sawed through the supporting beams.

The handwritten will of a Texas farmer named Herman
Oberweiss indicated beyond a shadow of a doubt what he
thought of his brother Oscar. It was first printed in a Texas
newspaper, and has cropped up in various places since. However, it is so funny it deserves to be included as a classic
example of a vindictive will. Here it is, verbatim:

I am writing of my will mineself that des lawyir
want he should have so much money he ask to many
answers about the family. First think i want done i
dont want my brother Oscar to get a god dam thing.
I got he is a musser he done me out of four dollars
fourteen years since.

I want it that Hilda my sister she gets the north
sixtie akers of at where I am homing it now i bet she
dont get that loafer husband of hers to brake twenty
akers next plowing. She cant have it if she lets Oscar
live on it i want it should have it back if she does.

Tell mama that six hundret dollars she has been
looking for ten years is berried from the bakhouse behind about ten foot down. She is better lett little Frederick do the digging and count it when he comes
up.

Paston Licknitz can have three hundret dollars
if he kisses the book he wont preach no more dum-
head talks about politks. He should a roof put on the
meeting house with the elders should the bills look
at.

Mama should the rest get but i want it so that
Adolph should tell her what not she should do so no
more slick irishers sell her vaken cleaner they noise
like hell and a broom dont cost so much.

I want it that mine brother Adolph be my executor

and I want it that the judge should pleese make Adolph plenty bond put up and watch him like hell. Adolph is a good business man but only a dumkoph would trust him with a busted pfennig.

I want dam sure that Schleimiel Oscar dont nothing get tell Adolph he can have a hundret dollars if he prove to Judge Oscar dont get nothing; that dam sure fix Oscar.

John Crom, of Shamong, New Jersey, didn't have much money when he made out his will, but he had plenty of imagination. The full text reads: "I, John Crom, do hereby give and bequeath all of my personal property and real estate, including farms, cattle ranches, cranberry bogs, horses, railroads, steamship lines, oil wells, ocean cables, and my castle in Spain, also my castles in the air, to John D. Rockefeller, providing he can find them." The will was duly signed, executed, and offered for probate, despite its apparent worthlessness.

A bachelor farmer named Samuel Drake Warfield left his home town of Helena, Arkansas, $500,000 when he died in 1967, and the money had to be spent for free music. The bequest kept growing, and the town just dedicated a $1,000,000 auditorium at which Van Cliburn has already played. The townspeople are talking of bringing in the New York Philharmonic—pretty heady stuff for a town of 21,422 persons.

Clark Gable left his wife Kay $1,000,000 but he also took care of the first of his five wives, Josephine Dillon, because she's the one who taught him to act. He left her a home.

Vivien Leigh willed her eyes to an eye bank, but the offer was rejected because she suffered from tuberculosis.

A woman-hating man named T. M. Zink provided that his estate, valued at from $40,000 to $80,000, should go into a trust fund for seventy-five years. At that time the accumulated interest would bring the estate up to $3,000,000, to be used for building a womanless library named for himself. The words "No Woman Admitted" must be cut in stone over the main entrances of the library; only books by men will be allowed; magazines will be censored to eliminate articles by women. Nothing in the design, decoration, or appointments of the library must suggest feminine influence. The will left $5 to his daughter, Mrs. Margretta Becker, and provided that his widow is to have the use of the house as long as she desires it for $40 a month rent.

Harold Bowhay didn't have much truck with hippies, and made it clear in his will. Each of his sixteen grandchildren, grandnieces, and nephews was willed $1,999 if he or she avoids the hippie life. Otherwise the amount is just $1.

A retired Army master sergeant named Vartivos Tatosian left his entire hoard of $90,000 to the Bishop of the Orthodox Catholic Church, Capital of Armenia, Republic of Soviet Union, for "the use and benefit of all poor and orphaned Armenian children of his diocese." Tatosian died in San Francisco, but his lawyer thought there would be no problem in sending the money to Armenia.

Ian Baratinsky of Warsaw surprised his heirs by making his will in the form of a phonograph record, with his own voice dictating the terms in a lawyer's office after his death. The expectant heirs were even more shocked when they heard they had inherited nothing. The entire $55,000 estate was willed to Miss Eliza Kolchowska, daughter of Mme. Kolchowska, a Polish opera singer who had died fifteen years previously. Ian had never met Mme. Kolchowska or her daughter, but Madame's recordings had given him much pleasure.

Thomas Miller, a retired farmer of Lafayette, Indiana, lived on dried cornflakes and potato chips whenever his checking account went below $50,000, because he was worried about financial security in his old age. When he died in 1962, Miller left half a million dollars to the city of Lafayette, specifying that part of the proceeds should be used to build a new grade school bearing his name.

The two Baxter sisters of Harrogate, England, were willed $600 a month "if they kept men away from their door." Their brother William Henry Baxter, whose estate amounted to more than $1,000,000 and who made the strange bequest, apparently did not take into account the fact that his sisters were both in their seventies and were unlikely to have swains battering at the door in any event.

A noted Portland brain specialist bequeathed "a lusty belch" to 95 percent of his medical coworkers. Dr. Arthur J. McLean also bequeathed a dollar to anyone who should attempt to break the will. McLean specified there was to be no funeral service of any sort, that his body be cremated, and that his ashes be strewn on the Straits of San Juan de Fuca.

William Gillette, the great actor, built a big house fashioned like a medieval castle on a high bluff at Hadlyme, Connecticut, and then proceeded to have built three miles of narrow-gauge railroad on the grounds, complete with bridges, trestles, tunnels through solid rock, and stone culverts. He had a steam locomotive and an electric one, a railway shop, and a round-house. For fifteen years the train system was his greatest delight. In his will, Gillette specifically warned the executors against disposing of the estate to "some blithering saphead" who wouldn't appreciate it. He wanted somebody to get the property who was fitted by nature to get as much kick out of it as he had. Alas, the executors could find no buyer fitting Gillette's specifications and won the court's consent to sell the railroad separately and turn the castle and grounds over to the state for a state park.

Ventriloquist Edgar Bergen has willed $10,000 to the Actors Fund of America, with a proviso that at least $500 a year shall be used to entertain children in orphanages and hospitals with ventriloquist acts in which Charlie McCarthy is to be used as the dummy. For this purpose Charlie is to be kept in good and serviceable condition and repair.

Showman P. T. Barnum, always talkative, wrote a will fifty-three pages long, which he had published in book form. The will benefited circus people, old pals, newspapermen, charitable institutions, and Tufts College. Calvin Coolidge, always taciturn, also wrote a will in keeping with his character: It was only twenty-five words long.

The most surprising bequests in the will of humorist-publisher Bennett Cerf were the gifts of $1,000 each to Frank Sinatra, Claudette Colbert, and Kitty Carlisle Hart, and $500 to each of Kitty's two children. Cerf's two sons and his wife were willed the bulk of the estate of over $1 million.

A hastily scribbled note "to whomever discovers me after death" was singer Dorothy Dandridge's last will. It reads, "In case of death, don't remove anything I have on—scarf, gown or anything to wear. Cremate right away. If I have anything, money, furniture, give it to my mother who knows what to do." She gave the note to her manager, Earl Mills, who was the one who discovered her dead. He said she was bankrupt.

The will of movie producer Sam Wood required that his two daughters and their children and a household servant must take an oath of loyalty to the United States before receiving their bequests. Thus the will reiterated Wood's well-known opposition to communism and the Communist Party or any other party advocating communistic principles.

A love that reached beyond death was revealed in the will of Valentine Browne Lawless, who joined the Army Air Force several months after Pearl Harbor. He wanted one perfect rose sent every week to the girl he had loved for three years before the war, in the event he did not return. Lawless died in action, and his brother Edward, who was named executor, faithfully sent that one rose to Mildred Fitzpatrick. Mildred had married in the meantime and didn't really want that weekly rose from her former suitor, but that didn't deter Edward from carrying out his dead brother's wishes. When the story of this bequest became public, a Hearst newspaper used the story, along with a picture of Mildred. That didn't set well with Mildred either. She sued the paper for invasion of privacy, but lost the suit in an appellate court ruling.

A Belgian woman named Marietje De Bruycker left her entire estate of $400,000 worth of property to her tenants, on condition that each of them attend Mass every year and pray for her soul.

Among the items listed as comprising the estate of Senator Everett McKinley Dirksen were a package of "Big Smile" marigold seeds, twenty thousand newspaper clippings, bifocal glasses, a Bible, a metal figure of a trumpeting elephant, and $53,379 in unspent campaign funds. Dirksen had tried, unsuccessfully, to have the marigold named the national flower.

In the "coals to Newcastle" department, an oldtime juggling partner of W. C. Fields willed the comedian a case of scotch. The will of Claude C. Ferdinand directed his executors to permit Fields to select his own brand.

A Quincy collie named Lassie is dogged, even as you and I, by income taxes. Lassie was bequeathed $5,000 by her master. "Lassie must pay an inheritance tax," snarled state tax commissioner Henry F. Long of Massachusetts. The inheritance tax amounted to $369. "Lassie will also have to pay a tax annually on any income her $4,631 draws," Long added.

James H. Bedford, a teacher in Glendale, California, left $100,000 to the International Foundation for Cryogenics Research, Inc., with the stipulation that the firm freeze his body until science can bring him back to life. The will was contested by Bedford's twelve grandchildren, but was upheld by the Superior Court. So Bedford is happily floating frozen in a tank of liquid nitrogen somewhere in Arizona, while the grandchildren shiver.

Dolores Moran, an actress who was at one time a waitress, didn't even notice a man named Anthony Ponce when she served him coffee and a hamburger at a restaurant in San Jose, California. But then she was only fifteen at the time. Mr. Ponce not only noticed Dolores, but he remembered her well. Twenty-seven years later Ponce willed her a ten-acre orchard worth more than $250,000.

The double life of Julian Ellis-Morris, of Liverpool, England, didn't come to light until he died and his will was filed. Julian dressed like a tramp and sold razor blades, shampoo, and soap door-to-door. At night he returned to a luxurious bungalow where he had three TV sets and two automobiles, including a chauffeur-driven Daimler limousine. When he disappeared from his regular rounds for a few days every now and then he wasn't out getting more supplies to sell. He was in Paris, living it up with two girls at the Folies Bergère. Part of the fortune he left when he died at the age of seventy-five in 1967 went to his two Folies Bergère pals and to two women owners of Montmartre hotels where Julian stayed during his sprees.

Daniel K. Weiskopf didn't like his son-in-law worth a darn, and made it quite clear in his will. The will left his daughter Danise Reid one third of his $2,500,000 estate if she divorced her husband, Harris Reid. She could be married to anybody at all as long as it wasn't Reid, in order to receive the $30,000 annual income from her share of the estate.

Frederick ("Fritz") Loewe, who composed *My Fair Lady*, *Gigi*, and other musicals with his collaborator, Alan Jay Lerner, has willed the royalties from his show tunes to the Eisenhower Medical Center and the Desert Hospital at Palm Springs, California. The hospitals will share the money from *Brigadoon, Day Before Spring, Paint Your Wagon, Camelot*, and *Gigi*, and the royalties should bring in more than $1,000,-000. Mr. Loewe is still very much alive and well and living in Palm Springs, but if he ever gets sick he can be sure of good hospital care. One of Fritz's proudest possessions is a framed canceled check for $1,000,000, paid him for *My Fair Lady* by CBS.

John Quincy Murray of Los Angeles had some definite ideas concerning the deportment of the younger generation and the conduct of ministers, as evidenced in his will. He left $2,000 to granddaughter Jean Murray, provided she foreswore bobbed hair, cosmetics, jewelry, dances, and movies. His grandson Malcolm was left $1,000 if he promised never to wear a mustache, go to dances or movies, or join a secret society. The rest of the estate was left to the Free Methodist Church of North America, to be used for superannuated ministers' pensions, provided none of the ministers wear watch chains or their wives wrist watches.

A Harvard psychologist named Truman Lee Kelley, who spent a lifetime studying the human race and the improvement of same by selective breeding, left trust funds from his estate of $175,000 to his two sons on the condition that they and the wives they should select must score well on a series of mental-physical character tests. To qualify for the money, the sons and their prospective wives—before marrying—must give the trustees information required to determine the couple's "E" (for eugenics) score. The "E" score would be based on the couple's deviation above or below the American white population averages for health, intellect, and character. Each point above average would bring the son and his bride $400; each point below the average would result in a $400 deduction. The couples would get $600 a point for each child. Son Kalon said he agreed with his father's theories and intended to comply with the terms of the will. Son Kenneth wasn't so sure he wanted to select a wife solely on the standards imposed by his father. "I don't want to place money before marriage itself," he said.

Fireman Richard Gregory Shaw struck up a casual friendship with a New York writer named Bushnell Dimond, and the two often took walks together or stopped off for a beer. They had conversations for three years about art, literature, and world culture in general. Then they sort of drifted apart, and didn't see each other for thirteen years. One day Shaw stopped by the firehouse while off duty for a cup of coffee with the boys, and learned he was heir to $250,000 left him by his old acquaintance Dimond, who had died a few months previously. The firemen showed Shaw a copy of the New York *Daily News* containing an open letter from Dimond's attorney —the lawyer's only means of tracking Shaw down. Shaw's first move was to quit his moonlighting job as a taxi driver.

Philosophy, wit, and wisdom sparkle the will of author Gene Fowler. His greatest regret was that he had little financial protection for his beloved wife Agnes, as he wrote "for his own soul's satisfaction," not for money. In his will Fowler wrote, "The Grim Reaper has sharp elbows and is nudging me. . . . I need not apologize to my heirs for the fact that I have given such small attention to the material prizes of the world. . . . I dislike few men and can say in God's presence that I hate no man. Life has been good to me."

It took nearly twenty years to close the estate of Tom Mix, one of the first film cowboys. Originally estimated at $102,711, the estate had dwindled due to the claims of forty-four persons. The final accounting left nothing for Tom's wife Mabel and his daughter Thomasina, his heirs.

The will of Andrew Carnegie disposed of an estimated $30,000,000. Besides leaving all his real estate to his wife, he left specific legacies or annuities to fifty-six people, including six charities. It was not surprising that Carnegie provided handsomely for all who had been employed by him or his family, including the employees and farmers on the family estate. Somewhat surprising, however, were his bequests of $5,000 each to Mrs. Grover Cleveland and Mrs. Theodore Roosevelt, and $10,000 each to William Howard Taft and David Lloyd George. Perhaps this was Carnegie's way of emphasizing an often-expressed view that public servants were underpaid.

When the parents of a young man named Rudolph Kronman hired a pretty English housemaid named Victoria to work in their Boston home, Rudolph promptly got the young lady pregnant, married her, and a son, whom they named Walter, was born five months later. Victoria didn't like the attitude of her husband's parents and friends, and went back to England with the baby. Rudolph lost complete touch with her. A few years later Rudolph fell in love with a young lady named Marie Falcone, and since he couldn't find Victoria to divorce her, he went ahead and married Marie in the Catholic Church. Rudolph and Marie had an idyllic married life, three children and four grandchildren. During one of their numerous travels Kronman died, at the age of seventy-four. Somehow his first son Walter, now middle-aged and living in England, heard of his father's death. He and his mother Victoria immediately came to America to claim the estate, with marriage and birth certificates in hand, as proof. Marie and the three children, one of whom was a nun, didn't want the scandal of lengthy litigation, so Victoria got the widow's third of the estate. Marie's three children were considered by the courts to be legitimate, despite the bigamous marriage, so they and Walter shared equally in the remaining two thirds of the estate. Marie got nothing. Victoria and Walter returned to England $200,-000 richer.

Harry F. Guggenheim, publisher, philanthropist, and ambassador to Cuba under President Hoover, left over $12,000,000 to charity. His forty-eight-page will, executed in 1970, also provided for three daughters, a son-in-law, and a cousin. However, Guggenheim had second thoughts about a bequest of $100,000 he made to Bill Moyers, former press secretary to President Johnson, plus 20 percent of his interest in various mining companies. These bequests were withdrawn in a codicil dated just two months later.

H. L. Mencken, author, editor, and journalist, left his letters to the New York Public Library with the proviso that they not be made public for fifteen years. Thirty thousand letters and notes were involved, including letters from William Faulkner, F. Scott Fitzgerald, Theodore Dreiser, Sinclair Lewis, Clarence Darrow, Helen Keller, and Kaiser Wilhelm. Mencken willed his diary to the Enoch Pratt Free Library of Baltimore, to be made available in 1981.

J. Howard Pew, chairman of the Sun Oil Company, left a will, executed in 1963, naming the J. Howard Pew Freedom Trust a principal beneficiary of his estimated $100 million estate. His will expressed a desire for privacy, which was one of Pew's chief traits during his lifetime. He had always refused to make public his private affairs and philanthropies. His will expressed the wish that the inventory and appraisement of his estate not be filed for public inspection, but be made only for the benefit of his estate and those interested in it. He exonerated his executor from responsibility for failure to file an inventory or appraisement.

Former U. S. senator Edward Long, Democrat of Missouri, changed his will three weeks before his death in the fall of 1972, reducing his wife's and daughter's share and leaving the bulk of his estimated $2,300,000 estate to his secretary of 26 years, Helen Dunlop. He allegedly made the change be-

A *Miscellany of Interesting Wills* 213

cause of a family quarrel. His wife had filed for separate maintenance, but no hearing had been held. The will left $10 each
to his wife and daughter, and Mrs. Long inherited the couple's
thirty-two-room home on a 345-acre farm near Clarksville,
north of St. Louis, and other properties.

Helen Dunlop, as trustee, was given the power and authority to manage the Long holdings, including 2 banks, 21 small-
loan companies, and nearly 2,000 acres of farmland. She was
also authorized to continue the operation of Senator Long's
corporate and other business interests.

Miss Dunlop and Long's daughter are each to be paid from
trust income an annual allowance of $7,500, in addition
to Miss Dunlop's remuneration in connection with operating
the business enterprises. On the death of Miss Dunlop and
Long's daughter, the entire income from the trust goes to
Long's five-year-old granddaughter, who will receive half of
the trust at age 25 and the remainder at age 30. The will
stressed that Long's son-in-law could at no time serve as a
trustee if a vacancy occurs.

Long's widow, Florence, filed a $3,250,000 suit charging
Miss Dunlop with alienation of her husband's affections, and
also petitioned the court to determine the assets of his estate,
claiming that Miss Dunlop and two other employees "have
concealed or embezzled or otherwise unlawfully held" property owned by the late senator.

Right on top of that suit, Miss Dunlop touched off an official
probe by charging that Long's death was actually the result
of poisoning. She claimed that before Long died he told her
he had eaten some chocolates sent to him by a businessman
in Clayton, Missouri, and thought he had been poisoned by
it, as it had a bitter taste. The businessman denied sending
candy to Long, and Miss Dunlop did not say why she waited
four months after Long's death to tell her story to authorities.

Famous American dress designer Norman Norell had a soft
spot for the school that taught him his craft. He willed his
half-million-dollar estate to a friend named John Moore, Jr.,
of Alice, Texas, with the proviso that on Moore's death the

estate goes to the Parsons School of Design in New York, where Norell was a student.

Charles Atlas, whose claim to fame was his system of body development, left his son Charles, Jr., $20,000 with the hope he would comply with his parents' wishes and be baptized as a Roman Catholic. Each of his three grandsons was left $10,-000, with the request they be baptized in the Roman Catholic Church also.

Besides bequests to the San Francisco Symphony and Opera and to the deYoung Museum, Helen deYoung Cameron, daughter of the founder of the San Francisco *Chronicle*, left eight heirs—nieces and nephews—$80,000 each. Mrs. Cameron was very fond of her pink stucco Mediterranean house called "Rosecourt," in Burlingame, and wanted her heirs to have the priceless furnishings of the house. However, instead of giving them the right of selection, as President Roosevelt did, she stipulated that the heirs should bid against each other for what they wanted.

Joseph Valachi, former Mafioso turned government informant, died in a federal prison in El Paso while serving a life sentence for murdering a fellow inmate he thought had been sent by Vito Genovese to kill him. Valachi left his entire estate of between $5,000 and $10,000 to a forty-five-year-old woman named Miss Jackson, of Niagara Falls, New York, with whom he had corresponded for five years before his death, but whom he had never met. But that was only the beginning of Miss Jackson's legacy. Royalties for *The Valachi Papers*, written by Peter Maas with information provided by Valachi, keep coming into the estate. So far $30,000 in royalties has gone to the estate, of which one half was taken by the government for back taxes. Miss Jackson also received her share of the movie rights to the book. She was named executrix of the estate, and she is the one who claimed Valachi's body and had it buried in upstate New York.

When Martin Eggers reported to work at the factory one morning in the 1940s, his coworkers greeted him with the news that he was an heir. One of them had heard a radio show called "Court of Missing Heirs," during which it was said an old man named Martin Eggers had died leaving an estate of $175,000 and that no heirs could be found. Because of the same rather unusual name they, and Martin, assumed the deceased must be Martin's father. The senior Eggers had separated when Martin was a very young child, and neither Martin nor his mother had ever heard of or seen the father again. They looked into the matter and learned that old man Eggers had lived in a single room in Brooklyn and was such a miser he went to a local synagogue for free meals. His large hoard of money had been found after his death. But they could find no proof that the dead Eggers was indeed their husband and father. Martin's lawyer unearthed some notes the old man had written. Then he asked Martin if he had anything with his father's writing on it—had he ever received a letter or card from his father? Martin remembered he had received a postcard from his father shortly after his parents' separation, but had no idea whether he still possessed the card or not. The lawyer suggested he make a search. After several days of relentless searching through all his effects, Martin finally found the card in a book. He triumphantly presented the card to the lawyer, the writing on the card was compared with the writing on the old man's notes, and a holographic expert decided both were written by the same person. So Martin did actually become an heir.

Thomas A. Edison's will bequeathed the bulk of his $12,-000,000 estate to his two sons, Charles and Theodore, by his second wife; the sons were also named executors of the will. The will empowered the executors to transfer to a trust company all of his bonds, and stipulated that the income therefrom should be divided equally among his six children: Marion Edison Oser, Thomas A. Edison, Jr., William L. Edison, Madeleine Edison Sloane, Charles Edison, and Theodore M. Edison. This will was executed February 1, 1926. In a codicil dated July 30, 1931, Edison bequeathed to his two sons Charles and Theodore all his shares of the preferred capital stocks of Edison Cement Corporation, to be divided equally between them.

All the serial debenture notes issued by the Edison Cement Corporation were to be divided among the six children in this manner: Charles and Theodore were to receive 40 percent each, and the other four children were to receive 5 percent each. William Edison, a son of Edison's first wife, contested the codicil of the will by alleging undue influence. The codicil was executed when Edison was eighty-four years old, three months before his death. William claimed that the difference between the original will and the codicil would be $130,000 annually, his estimate of what he would receive through the unfair codicil, and $650,000 annually, the amount he estimated he was bequeathed in the original fair will.

The fact that a secretary can become as valuable to a man as members of his family was well illustrated in the will of Albert Einstein. He willed his secretary, Helena Dukas, $20,-000, the same amount he willed his stepdaughter Margot Einstein, while his son Edward Einstein received only $15,000 and his son Albert Einstein, Jr., received $10,000. Helena was also willed Einstein's books, personal clothing, and personal effects, except his violin. The violin was bequeathed to grandson Bernhard Caesar Einstein. Helena Dukas and Margot Einstein were given control of the remainder of the estate, with this specification: "It is to be borne in mind that my primary object is to make further provision for the care, comfort and welfare of my secretary Helena Dukas during her lifetime; my secondary object is to make such further provision for the care, comfort and welfare of my step-daughter Margot Einstein during her lifetime; my final object is that any property which may remain shall pass to the Hebrew University."

Among the thirty-one specific bequests in the will of J. P. Morgan, dated January 4, 1913, was a bequest of $250,000 to Mary G. McIlvaine, "friend." Just two days after executing the will, Morgan executed, on January 6, 1913, a codicil to the will stipulating that in lieu of the legacy bequeathed to Mary G. McIlvaine, she was to receive an annual income of $25,000. That was the sole provision of the codicil. One can't help wondering what could have happened during those two days to make Morgan change his mind. Did Mary go on a wild spending spree that made Morgan fear she would blow the whole legacy? Did Mary request the change herself, for tax purposes? The events of those two days does tickle the imagination.

Paul Revere had similar second thoughts and reservations regarding the $4,000 he bequeathed each of his daughters Mary, Harriett, and Maria in his will dated November 15, 1816. In a codicil dated March 14, 1818, Revere stipulated that instead of receiving the $4,000 each, the three daughters were only to receive the interest on the $4,000 during their natural lives. After the death of each daughter, her heirs were to receive the $4,000 outright. Each of Revere's grandchildren was willed $500, with one exception: "It is my will that my grandson Frank (who now writes his name Francis Lincoln) eldest son of my late daughter Deborah shall have no part of my estate, except one dollar which is here bequeathed to him." Goodness, was Revere *that* mad because Frank started calling himself Francis?

John D. Rockefeller left the bulk of his estimated $25,000,000 estate to his granddaughter, Mrs. Margaret Strong de Cuevas, her children, and the Rockefeller Institute for Medical Research, in his will dated June 2, 1925. Some question must have arisen as to why Margaret and her children were favored over the other grandchildren and their descendants. In any event, Rockefeller answered the question in the third codicil to his will, dated October 3, 1934, with this statement: "I am getting up this trust for the benefit of my granddaughter Margaret and her descendants to the exclusion of my other grandchildren and their descendants because, when the time came that I felt it wise to place upon my children the responsibility of owning and administering substantial sums and for that purpose made large gifts to or for them, my oldest daughter Bessie, the mother of my granddaughter Margaret, was not living."

It has been a continuing source of wonder and amusement that William Shakespeare's only bequest to his wife was his second-best bed. He seems to have had considerable property

when he died, the major portion of which went to his two
daughters, Susanna and Judith. Susanna and her husband John
Hall were made executrix and executor, respectively, of the
will. Shakespeare's only gesture toward leaving money to charity was a contribution of ten pounds to the poor of Stratford.
He left five friends twenty-six shillings and eight pence each
with which to buy rings for themselves. For some reason a
sixth friend was left only twenty-six shillings, without that extra eight pence, with which to buy his ring. Was that to indicate his lower rating in Shakespeare's echelon of friends?

The foremost desire expressed in George Washington's will
was that all his slaves should receive their freedom upon his
wife's death. Those who were too old and infirm or too young
to support themselves after being given freedom were to be
comfortably clothed and fed by Washington's heirs. His will
provided for "the immediate freedom of my mulatto man William (calling himself William Lee); or if he should prefer it
(on account of the accidents which have befallen him, and
which have rendered him incapable of walking or of any active employment) to remain in the situation he now is, it shall
be optional in him to do so. In either case I allow him an an-
nuity of $30 during his natural life, which shall be independent
of the victuals and clothes he has been accustomed to receive
. . . this I give him as a testimony of my sense of his attachment to me, and for his faithful service during the Revolutionary War." Washington's humanitarianism was further
evidenced by his bequest of $4,000 in trust to the Academy
in Alexandria "for the purpose of educating such orphan children, or the children of such other poor and indigent persons
as are unable to accomplish it with their own means and who,
in the judgment of the trustees of said Seminary are best
entitled to the benefit of this donation." Also, because "it has
always been a source of serious regret with me to see the
youth of these United States sent to foreign countries for the
purpose of education, often before their minds were formed,
or they had imbibed any adequate ideas of the happiness of
their own;—contracting, too frequently, not only habits of dis-

sipation and extravagance, but principles unfriendly to Republican Government and to the true and genuine liberties of mankind; which, therefore are rarely overcome," Washington bequeathed in perpetuity fifty shares of stock in the Potomac Company toward the endowment of a university to be established in the District of Columbia under the auspices of the federal government. Thus was born George Washington University.

Douglas McKelvy, who became a millionaire through inheritance, died at the age of forty-one, in 1973, from liver complications caused by heavy drinking. Even as he made out his will he was thinking with pleasure of his two favorite New York pubs, Chez Madison and Gregory's Corner. He left $12,-000 to buy free liquor for patrons at those two bars, leaving the rest of his fortune to his two children. Before he died he told the manager of one of the pubs what a charge he got from the thought of his pals having a drink on him after his death. Since the pals were not named in the will, it took the executor of the estate and the bartenders of both pubs several months to figure out how to dispense the bequest.

A former actor named Charles McCarthy hired a practical nurse to care for his wife of fifty years when she became ill. After his wife's death the nurse refused to leave. In fact, she stayed on until McCarthy, then in his eighties, died. McCarthy had written three wills after his wife died. In the first he left everything to the nurse, and a new lawyer he'd hired was named executor. In the second will, the nurse got everything and was named executrix. In the third will he left everything to his wife. He had married the nurse in the meantime. Actors' Equity probated the will, which was contested by the public administrator because the marriage was questionable and relatives were unknown. A jury decided that McCarthy lacked testamentary capacity when he made out the last will, and that the nurse, by then his wife, had used undue influence on him. The will was thrown out, which meant McCarthy had died intestate. Eventually his $100,000 estate was divided between the nurse and charity.

The smell of gas led neighbors to investigate the apartment of a couple we'll call Murphy. Mr. Murphy, who had previously suffered a stroke, was lying dead on the floor, with the dead body of his wife lying across him. The gas jets in the kitchen were turned on full force. The question arose as to which one had died first. If Mr. Murphy died first, his estate went to his wife and thence to her relatives. If Mrs. Murphy died first, her estate went to her husband and thence to his relatives. An ambulance doctor was paid by Mrs. Murphy's relatives to say that when he arrived on the scene, the body of Mr. Murphy was stone cold and the body of Mrs. Murphy was still warm, which meant he died first. Mr. Murphy's relatives talked to the police who were called in at the time of the discovery of the bodies; the police testified that both bodies were cold when they arrived. It was finally assumed that since Mr. Murphy had a stroke and was unable to go into the kitchen to turn on the gas jets, Mrs. Murphy had murdered her husband and committed suicide.

The estate of Emil Guth, which he willed to the sister of his dead wife, was denied probate because it was proved in a most interesting way that the two witnesses to the will did not sign the will at the time it was written by hand by Mr. Guth, but signed it after his death, which meant the witnesses falsified. The physical evidences existent on the paper on which the will was written showed that it had a smooth writing surface at the time the deceased wrote on it and that Guth's writings had dried completely while the paper was still smooth and its surface unbroken. Physical evidence also showed that the paper was thereafter folded or creased before any other writings were put upon it. It was a curious mischance that exposed the fraud. When the second witness wrote his name and address he made the stroke of the figure "1" diagonally across the then broken fabric of the paper, from repeated folding and unfolding. The ink from his pen ran into the crack not only above but below the point where the stroke of the "1" crossed the crease and also penetrated completely through the fabric of the paper and became visible on the back. The extent of absorption of ink into the crack of the paper left no possible doubt that the writing by this witness was not made contemporaneously with the writings by the deceased. This falsification was discovered and presented by former Judge Joseph A. Cox, and was what caused Surrogate Delehanty to deny probate of the will.

Actor Walter Huston left his actor-director son John nothing but a gold watch in his will, everything else going to his widow. His explanation for this was "John can always earn money."

Pablo Picasso knew what a scramble there would be among his legal heirs and claimants over his fortune when he died. He even predicted, "It will be worse than anything you can imagine." Thus he didn't even bother to make a will, and died intestate. His lawyer friend Armand Antebi said Picasso died without leaving a will because of his superstition about death. Some say he just wanted to be ornery. In any event, Picasso's prediction came true. He left an estimated $90,000,000 in bank accounts, investments, real estate, art works, etc. Besides all that, there is the incalculable treasure of his own works stored in his many homes, which include a forty-room castle in Vauvenargues, Provence, and his country mansion near Grasse. His biographer Sir Rowland Penrose said Picasso kept hundreds, possibly even thousands of his paintings, drawings, and sculptures. There are two known legal heirs to this vast fortune: his second wife Jacqueline, who married him in 1961, and Paulo Picasso, his fiftyish son by his first marriage to Russian dancer Olga Kolgova. Françoise Gilet, his former mistress who bore two illegitimate children of Picasso's, Claude and Paloma, and who is now very respectably married to polio vaccine discoverer Dr. Jonas Salk, let it be known that she expects her children to fight for a share of the estate. Claude and Paloma and an older illegitimate half sister have all been to court seeking to be recognized as Picasso's legitimate offspring. If the suits of all the claimants fail, Picasso's widow Jacqueline is entitled to half of all that her husband acquired since their marriage in 1961, and Paulo, the painter's only legitimate child, will inherit the remainder of the estate.

Everyone was surprised when the will of former surrogate judge of New York Robert Ludlow Fowler turned up with no witnesses' names on the will. What, surely a surrogate judge would know a will needed witnesses! But it turned out that Judge Fowler knew his business after all. Judge Fowler died in Westchester County in 1936, but his last will and testament in his own handwriting had been executed at Beaulieu-sur-Mer in France in 1932. After Fowler's retirement from the bench in 1919, he resided in France, and made out his holographic will while residing there. According to the laws of France, a holographic will written there does not require witnesses. The will was admitted to probate by the Surrogate's Court of Westchester County on the grounds that "a will executed without the State in the mode prescribed by the law, either of the place where executed or of the testator's domicile, shall be deemed to be legally executed."

The Metropolitan Museum of Art received the largest gift in its hundred-year history when it was willed the art collection of investment banker Robert Lehman—a collection that was started by Philip Lehman sixty years ago and continued by his son Robert. Valued at $100,000,000, the collection comprised nearly three thousand objects of Western European art, ranging from Botticelli, Bellini, and Rembrandt masterpieces to bronzes, tapestries, drawings, Limoges enamels, Venetian glass, furniture, and jewelry, mainly from the fourteenth to the nineteenth centuries. The acquisition touched off a storm of controversy when the Metropolitan proposed to house the collection in a new $8,000,000 wing to be built on fourteen thousand square feet of Central Park land. Lehman had wished the collection to be kept all together in one place, but couldn't have foreseen the protests by conservationists, angry citizens, and politicians over the chosen site. However, the Metropolitan held a lease on the park land and proceeded with construction after the suits of two complaining groups were dismissed.

The two men who were at Sir Noel Coward's bedside when he died and who had shared his life for thirty-five years inherited the bulk of his $25,000,000 estate. They were ex-chorus boy Graham Payne and Cole Lesley, Coward's valet and personal assistant. As well as the money, they also get the vastly lucrative royalty rights to all Coward's shows and songs.

Eleanora Sears, a great-great-granddaughter of Thomas Jefferson and a leading socialite in both Boston and Palm Beach until her death at the age of eighty-seven in 1968, left a large part of her multimillion-dollar estate to Miss Marie V. Gendron, an employee of Miss Sears at the time of her death, after the granting of a few special bequests.

Socialite-heiress Dorothy Gould Burns, granddaughter of railroad tycoon Jay Gould, was thinking fondly of a Frenchman named Jean Pierre Binello, "a friend," when she made out her will. She left him a Riviera villa, a Mercedes limousine, and $100,000 cash. She was fifty-eight and a widow when she died in 1968 at Juan-les-Pins, a Riviera resort town founded by her father, Frank Jay Gould. The bulk of her estate was divided equally among her three daughters, and she also left bequests of $10,000 each to two New York women, longtime friends of the family.

The surprising chief beneficiary of Maurice Chevalier's will was a former actress named Odette Melier, forty, who had appeared in a revue with Chevalier twenty years earlier and met him again by chance in 1968. After that chance meeting the two became close friends, and Odette and her crippled daughter Pascale moved to a Paris suburb to be near Chevalier's luxurious villa, La Louque. The villa was among the assets bequeathed to Odette.

George F. Getty, son of oil billionaire J. Paul Getty, left a handwritten will dated only five days before his mysterious death in June 1973, from alcohol and barbiturate poisoning. The strangest bequest in his will was a gift of $10,000 to his father, already one of the richest men in the world. He also left a $50,000 bequest to his former wife Gloria Gordon Getty, and a family trust to be divided among his wife, mother, stepfather, and three daughters.

The death of Mrs. Horace Dodge, one of the world's richest women, at the age of 103 in 1970, resulted in the reopening of several tangled court battles among her grandchildren and great-grandchildren for shares of her estate, estimated to be in excess of $100,000,000. She married Horace Dodge in 1896, when Horace was a mechanic, and by the time Horace died in 1920 he was making Dodge cars and left his wife $59,000,000, which she put into tax-free municipal bonds. The money was said to have earned an average of $1,500,000 a year, and Mrs. Dodge never had to pay a federal income tax. Over the years she was embroiled in several court actions stemming from her husband's provisions for his children and grandchildren.

On her death, Mrs. Dodge's estate was to be divided between the two Dodge children, Horace, Jr., and Delphine. In the meantime, millions were spent ironing out the marital problems of Delphine, who was married three times, and Horace, Jr., who was married five times. Mrs. Dodge outlived both her children. Delphine died in 1943, after stipulating in her will that her share of the estate be divided between her daughters, Mrs. Anna Ray Baker Ranger and Christine Cromwell Christensen. At one point Christine sued her grandmother on grounds of mismanagement of the estate. Horace Dodge, Jr., produced five children in his five marriages, and died while in the process of divorcing Gregg Sherwood Dodge, a former showgirl and mother of his youngest son, John. Gregg sued the estate for $11,000,000 and settled out of court for $9,000,000.

Detroit officials estimated that seven of Mrs. Dodge's grandchildren would inherit as much as $20,000,000 each when the estate was finally settled.

It caused quite a stir in the newspapers when "millionaire big-game hunter Alfredo Cernadas" shot and killed his wife Patricia and himself in 1969. His will dated August 4, 1967, bequeathed half of Cernadas' estate to his wife Patricia "if she survives me." If Cernadas survived Patricia, the will stated, Patricia's share was to go into the residuary estate, bequeathed to Cernadas' two daughters and a son by a previous wife. The will directed the same disposition "if my wife and I shall die in a common disaster, or if for any reason it shall be difficult to determine the question of survivorship." It was believed that interesting legal questions would arise involving disposition of Cernadas' "vast estate." However, no questions of that nature arose, as it was soon discovered that Cernadas had died bankrupt and having many debts. This was surprising, as Cernadas' father in South America was reputed to be a multimillionaire, and Cernadas had once been married to Irene Wrightsman (by whom he had the children), the daughter of millionaire Charles B. Wrightsman of Palm Beach.

A house painter named Frank L. Chase, who lived in Norwalk, Connecticut, for sixty of his eighty-two years, lived quietly and frugally, but meantime built up a fortune through real estate and stock market investments, bequeathed the city of Norwalk his $250,000 when he died in 1963. He had outlived his wife, daughter, friends, and even one of the executors of his will, and remarked that since he made his money in Norwalk, he wanted it to stay there.

Donaldson Brown, who died in 1965 at his five hundred-acre estate near Port Deposit, Maryland, was an unwitting benefactor of his home state of Maryland. He left an estate estimated at $300,000,000, out of which estate and inheritance taxes to Maryland amounted to approximately $22,000,000. According to Maryland state comptroller Louis Goldstein, that $22,000,000 was sufficient at the time—1966—to balance the state budget. It was the largest will ever filed in Maryland history.

Canadian publisher Max Bell spent his last days before his death in 1972 at the Montreal Neurological Hospital, and was so pleased with the treatment he received there he willed the institution $750,000. His wife received $670,726, his mother was willed $24,074, a former wife was bequeathed $52,467, two daughters each received $133,219, son Paul got $259,526, brother Gordon came into $25,000, one sister received $12,694, and another sister got only $5,000. The principal beneficiary was the Bell Foundation, which received 200,000 common shares of FP Publications, valued at $14,000,000. After the other bequests, the Bell Foundation also received the remainder of the estate, $5,979,479.

A kindly spinster named Elizabeth Browning took a liking to a suave White Russian noble known as Baron Gregory von Zeitzoff, and kept him in style at the Waldorf for many years. When she died at the age of eighty-five she left the baron the income from a $7,500,000 trust fund. Gregory died three months later, and turned out to be neither a baron nor even a Zeitzoff. He was just plain Gregory Zaitseff.

A man-bites-dog story is that of John C. Burnett, a retired physician of Las Vegas, Nevada, who refused in common pleas court to accept an estimated $5,600,000 trust fund left him by his late wife Cora Timken Burnett. The fund would have netted him $800,000 a year for life, but Burnett refused it on the grounds that his wife had already amply provided for him. The trustee, the Cleveland Trust Company, brought suit to have the court decide what should be done with the trust fund after Dr. Burnett's refusal to accept it. The money was turned over to the Timken Foundation. Mrs. Burnett was the daughter of the founder of Timken Roller Bearing Company.

Nine women divided the jewelry of their late departed hostess and then toasted her with champagne at a bizarre luncheon. The hostess, Mrs. Alexandra Desbien, had died two months previously and provided for the luncheon in her will. She instructed the executors to invite the friends to the luncheon and let each guest take her turn choosing items from a display table. The guests had three choices of jewelry, including diamond rings, bracelets and brooches, and one choice each of cut glass items, china, and furniture. The estate paid the taxes on all items.

Mrs. Desbien's funeral provided a surprise too. The last rites were held at her hillside home. After her friends had arrived, Mrs. Desbien's voice thanked everyone for kindness and friendship. Only Mrs. Desbien and her executor knew about the phonograph record, which she had made for her funeral.

Among other things, Mrs. Desbien's will also left twenty-five shares of Oahu Plantation common stock to her mailman, Jimmy Ishimoto, "for many kindnesses shown me"; prohibited any autopsy following her death; and added, "death will be from natural causes, and if an accident, due to my carelessness."

Kenneth Hunnisett, a former chauffeur and now a mechanic, became the sudden owner of four automobiles, without so much as a one-car garage. The late Mrs. Bown Ismay, of London, for whom he was chauffeur for thirty-five years, left him two Rolls-Royces, one Hillman, and one Morris. "I'll have to sell three of them," he said, "and park the other on the road."

Eight prominent men were chosen by millionaire John Gaty to meet once a year to dispose secretly of $80,000 for charity. Gaty's will provided that $11,000 be given each year to each of the eight. Each must donate $10,000 to his favorite charity and keep $1,000 as a fee.

The eight men chosen were columnist William F. Buckley, Jr., FBI Director J. Edgar Hoover, Senators Strom Thurmond, John Tower, and Frank Lausche, Dean Clarence Manion of the Notre Dame Law School, Harding College president George Benson, and Edgar Eisenhower. As members died, the remaining members fill the vacancy with other men of their choosing. The group administers a $1,500,000, ten-year, self-liquidating trust fund.

W. C. Fuller, a yard man for more than twenty-five years, startled his customers by buying a $9,000 Cadillac and stopping by every Sunday to "inspect" their hedges and lawns before trimming them later in the week. He startled them even more when he died leaving a $100,000 trust fund to educate black youngsters, orphaned or from broken homes, in landscape architecture.

True to his professional avocation, a former newspaperman named Joseph D. Heade left a will asking that his pallbearers be supplied with "two fifths of potable whiskey" after his funeral. Heade's widow Henrietta said her husband's request could not be fulfilled because "the pallbearers are too old and can't drink any more." Obviously the pallbearers were not newspapermen.

In Worthington, England, two young men inherited $280 each from the will of a woman whose lost purse they had returned ten years before. The purse only had $5.60 in it.

When Wolfram von Pannwitz, a Lutheran member of the Prussian nobility and a career officer in the German Army, came to this country from Berlin in 1947, he lived modestly in a $23-a-week, 12 x 9 room in a hotel at 29th Street and Madison Avenue in Manhattan. He made a fortune in the stock market, and when he died he left an estate of $500,000. His will directed that half of it go to "Cardinal Spellman or his successor to employ the assets to help needy and deserving people of the community." He added, "In St. Patrick's Cathedral my prayers gave me always the strength and the power to accomplish the hard struggle for this life." The other half of his estate was left to the Hebrew Immigrant Aid Society to be used "for the purpose of assisting needy and deserving Jewish immigrants to the U.S. Three times during my life my Jewish friends in Europe and the United States gave me professionally decisive lifts and enabled me to make a decent living. As my Jewish friends are rich or at least well-to-do themselves, this is the best way to show my gratitude."

Edwin Orlando Swain, a tall, distinguished-looking gentleman of the old school who ran a voice culture studio, left a legacy rich in wit and elfin humor, though he may have died penniless. Three days after he gave a party for his eighty-second birthday he was dead, and his will was found by the police in his apartment, decorated with a red ribbon and a gold seal. The will contained only seven stipulations:

1. I direct that all my creditors be paid except my landlord. 2. I give and bequeath to my good friend, Theodore Weber, my best aluminum tin if I die of anything but indigestion. In that event I give him a

sad farewell. 3. To my old friend Ann Lewis, I give and bequeath Purcell's "Passing By," which I wrongfully took and carried away last Christmas. 4. I give and bequeath to my dear friend Mrs. George Hale the satisfaction of being remembered in my will. 5. To my old pal Mary Ledgerwood, I give and bequeath the sum of 35¢. It's not much but it's the beginning of a Scotch fortune. 6. I leave to my lawyer Huber Lewis the task of explaining to my relatives why they didn't get a million dollars apiece. 7. I appoint Huber Lewis executor of my will. In view of his profession I suppose we had better require him to furnish a bond. I give him full power to sell, mortgage or pledge any or all of my estate for the purpose of paying the legacy left by article 5, and if a sufficient sum cannot be realized, I warn him to be wary of the legatee.

The will was witnessed by three singers: the famous Madame Schumann-Heink, Louise Lurch, and Maria DeKyser. Preceding their signatures was this echo of *The Mikado:*

> Three little maids from school are we,
> Called to witness this will, you see
> And testify to its propriety,
> Three little maids from school.
> Everything has been properly done,
> But he knew right enough we considered it fun,
> Three little maids from school.

The will of Joseph Morris, ninety, who died after being arrested as a beggar, remembered his friend Morrison McMullen and his niece Jean. But court officials where the will was probated had a hard time trying to decide which one got the bulk of his $60,000 estate. It all depended on whether at a certain point in the handwritten will the punctuation mark was a period or a comma.

Thirteen turned out to be a lucky number for marrying

Tommy Manville's thirteenth wife, Christina. When Tommy died, Christina lost a husband but gained an estimated $30,-000,000. It was later discovered that Tommy had completely forgotten a $1,000,000 trust fund left to him by his father and had neglected to mention it in his will. Christina moved in to collect that last million too, but was foiled. In a five-part decision handed down by Surrogate Samuel DiFalco, he ruled that particular money could only be inherited by a blood relative. Accordingly, the million went to his niece Lorraine Manville Amato, daughter of Tommy's sister Lorraine. Oddly enough, when Tommy's sister had died four years previously, she too had forgotten her $1,000,000 trust. It eventually went to her daughter.

Three minutes meant a fortune to a shapely teen-ager in Italy named Anna Maria Casati. Her father, the Marquis Camillo Casati Stampa Di Soncino, shot his wife Anna and her handsome lover Massimo Minorenti, then committed suicide—a case that shocked Italian society and made headlines for weeks. A medical legal expert reported that Anna died of two rifle wounds in the chest, which killed her almost instantly, while the marquis, shooting himself with the same rifle after reloading it, wounded himself twice in the throat and died more slowly, bleeding to death from a bullet-torn jugular vein. It was decided he had died three minutes after his wife Anna, to whom he had willed all his possessions. Had the marquis died first, then the parents of the murdered wife, Signor and Signora Ernesto Fallarino, would have inherited the entire Casati estate. With Anna dying first, the estate willed to her automatically reverted to the still-living marquis, cutting off her relatives from any further claim. The Casati fortune then went to the nearest kin, Marquisina Anna Marie Casati. The vast fortune included estates, villas, farms, vineyards all over Italy, a forty-room palace in Milan, a private island off Anzio, and a famous stable of racing horses at Varese.

Jacob Franks, the father of little Bobby Franks, who was brutally murdered by Nathan Leopold and Richard Loeb in Chicago, carried his bitterness against his son's murderers to the grave. His will set aside money for a lawyer to protest, if ever the murderers came up for parole, "a lenient governor, a shrewd lawyer, there are many ways they could be put at liberty." Loeb was murdered in prison by another inmate. Leopold, who was always considered to have been a tool in Loeb's hands, became a model prisoner, and became such an expert on the handling and reading of X-rays he was considered invaluable by the prison, and was much respected. Even Jacob Franks would probably not have objected when Leopold was finally released from prison, after thirty-odd years, and moved to Puerto Rico, where he died.

Walter C. Wyland of Los Angeles liked to brag that he had accounts in seventy banks all over the world. His will, written on the back of an old calendar hanging on the wall, left his estate to his fiancée, Mrs. Doris Vroubel. Imagine her surprise when she discovered that the faraway bank accounts totaled only $400, since he had opened them with small amounts by mail and many had been closed out for service charges.

Comedian Joe Laurie, Jr., wrote in his will that he was "of sound mind although being an actor and writer." He stipulated that his ashes be strewn in the fireplace of the Lambs Club on West 44th Street in New York "some day when the fire is roaring." If this was not permitted, he asked that his ashes be placed in the resin box of the Palace Theatre; a resin box is used by performers before going onstage so their feet won't slip.

Alexander Hilton died when a Navy patrol plane on which he was a crewman during World War II plunged into the ocean 325 miles northwest of Guam. His body was not recovered. His mother, Mrs. Alexander Hilton, a former Army nurse from Aurora, Illinois, stipulated in her will that she wished to join her son in death. She was lowered into the sea in a ceremony by the crew of the Navy salvage ship *Conserver* at the same spot where her son had perished, as nearly as it could be pinpointed.

A wealthy Copenhagen businessman decided to visit his relatives before he died. All but one served him his favorite dish, chopped raw beef. One served him roast pork. Infuriated, he amended his will, canceling a bequest of $7,000 to the unfortunate relative who served him the wrong thing.

Mrs. Ada Biggs of England also had strong feelings about what was served her. She liked her tea "strong enough for a mouse to dance on." When she went to live with her son George in London, tea was still rationed and had to be used sparingly. Angered because George didn't make the tea strong enough, she cut him out of her will. The court decided this was inexcusable injustice, and George was named her heir.

Lucille Rutshaw sold corsages to sailors in San Diego for twenty years. They called her "the flower lady," and some gave her battle ribbons and badges, which she pinned to a velvet cushion. When she died in 1961 she willed that the cushion be buried with her. She also made arrangements in her will for charity to benefit from her estate. In 1972 the Bank of America turned over to charity the first ten years' interest of $72,000 on her $200,000 estate, which she had put in trust for that purpose.

In Patcham, England, a man who left $84,000 when he died hated tax collectors so much that his will read, "from my grave I curse the Board of Inland Revenue who have ruined my life." He asked that he be buried "outside the United Kingdom with my back to the country which I have served so well but which treated me and my family so badly."

In 1946 in Los Angeles, Mrs. Lucia Mitter left $25,000 to Sir Victor Sassoon, British financier. He was already worth $300,000,000.

French novelist Maurice Dekobra left his seventeen thousand books and works of art to the town of Papeete, Tahiti. His will said, "considering that gunpowder never prevented men from fighting but on the contrary encourages their worst instincts . . . I am convinced that the release of atomic energy means the total destruction of cities like Paris, London, Washington and New York." He hoped that more remote areas such as Tahiti would be spared.

When bachelor Arthur J. Macheck died in Milwaukee in

1945 he left $500 to Mrs. Clara Mohr Carcy for kisses she had given him in 1899, "the only kisses I ever received."

In Patrick Henry's speech in defense of the Colonies against England, his closing line was the immortal "Give me liberty or give me death." In his will he stipulated that his wife would have all his property only so long as she remained unmarried. Apparently Mrs. Henry felt as strongly about liberty as her husband had. She did remarry, and fought for her legal share of the estate in court.

Lawyers devised a game of cards to help a woman who could neither write nor speak to make her will. Two packs of cards were specially prepared. One contained the titles of her properties, and this was handled by the lawyer. The other pack bore the names of the woman's relatives. These cards she held herself. The game began with the lawyer laying down an "estate" card. The woman covered it with the card bearing the name of the relative she wished to inherit it. So the game went until the property had all been disposed of. The will was upheld in court.

The will of a man we will call John Doe bequeathed his widow Jane Doe half of his $3,000,000 estate. The other half went to his two stepchildren of a former marriage. After a short period of mourning, Mrs. Doe went into court to break the will, claiming that a few days prior to their marriage in August 1957, John had promised to will her everything. To prove her point, she introduced a letter purportedly written to her by John at that time. The letter directed that some $400,000 in securities held by "Merrill Lynch, Pierce, Fenner and Smith" be turned over to her. The stepchildren hired Carl Rubino, a lawyer, to defend their legacy. Doing his homework very well, Rubino came up with the fact that the firm known as Merrill Lynch, Pierce, Fenner and Beane had not changed its name using the name of Smith rather than Beane until December of 1957. Rubino hired investigators and uncovered an electric typewriter Mrs. Doe had sold to a friend in 1966. On the ribbon he was able to detect parts of letters and words matching words in the letter supposedly written nine years earlier. The stepchildren received their rightful legacy, and Mrs. Doe was arrested on a thirteen-count indictment charging grand larceny, forgery, and perjury.

In 1892 George Willis was brought to Joplin, Missouri, by his grandfather, James Connor, to select a birthday present for his fifth birthday. He requested a case of strawberry pop. The boy was very careful of his soda pop and only drank a bottle on special occasions. When Grandfather Connor heard of the child's frugality, he put in his will that if the boy attained the age of sixty-five and could produce one unopened bottle of the original twenty-four, he would inherit the $14,000 farm. On Willis' sixty-fifth birthday he still had three bottles, one of which he drank, one he dropped, and the other he presented to the probate court to receive title to the farm.

Paul von Hindenburg stated in his will that he desired reinstatement of the monarchy in Germany and did not want Hitler to succeed him as chief of state. Hitler withheld a portion of the will, creating the impression that Von Hindenburg wanted Hitler to head the Reich when he died in 1934. Later Franz von Papen testified that he had just handed the will to Hitler without reading it, and thus didn't know its contents.

One of the smallest wills was that of Paul Regan, prominent Oakland, California, consulting engineer, leaving his estate to his wife, Mary, when he died in 1954. He had scrawled his will on a piece of newspaper 2½″ x 3″ years before.

Major Peter Stapleton Shaw wrote thirty-three wills before his death in 1954. In the last one Shaw, a former member of Parliament, left his estate worth $112,000 to his friend, Miss Emily Hutchinson.

Actor Lon Chaney left his estate to his wife and son Creighton. He also left $1 to one Cleve Creighton Chaney. Nobody could figure out who Cleve Creighton Chaney was, but writer Adela Rogers St. Johns was curious enough to try to find out, as she was writing an article on Chaney. Following various leads, Adela finally found Cleve working in a field. It turned out Cleve was Chaney's first wife and the real mother of his son Creighton. Chaney had tried to make the world believe

Creighton was his son by his second wife, the one who inherited half of his estate, according to Adela. Chaney had followed the usual practice of bequeathing exactly $1 to someone who might try to sue the estate later.

The amounts left by socialite yachtsman Fuller E. Callaway III, heir to a Georgia textile fortune who died at the age of thirty-nine from an apparent overdose of sleeping pills, to his three wives were the exact reverse of the usual procedure. He willed $100,000 to his first wife, Wanda (throwing in an additional $10,000 for her husband, James D. Warren), $10,000 to his second wife, Pia Lindstrom (TV personality and daughter of Ingrid Bergman), and only $1 to his third wife, former New York stage actress and Texas beauty queen Annette Cash. His original will had left $100,000 to Annette, but was amended a year later to leave her $1. Callaway's only child, Mark Callaway Warren, fifteen, was left his choice of $200,000 or half of Callaway's estate of $500,000 in trust, as well as Callaway's mansion in Atherton, California.

Harold West of London was an extremely cautious banker, whose greatest fear was being buried alive. His will specified that after he died his doctor was to drive a steel stake through his heart to make sure he was dead, and that when he was buried the coffin was not to be nailed shut in case he was not dead and he could thus escape. These strange stipulations were carried out when Mr. West died in 1972 at the age of ninety.

Nobody believed it or paid much attention when a little old lady in Boise, Idaho, put an advertisement in the paper to sell a 1969 Cadillac in first-class condition with low mileage for the sum of $50. Finally somebody nibbled and found it was true enough, with no gimmicks to trick the buyer. It turned out the little old lady had a good reason for offering the car at that price. She recently became widowed, and her late husband specified in his will that the car or the proceeds from the sale were to go to his girlfriend.

Otto Flick, a twenty-nine-year-old German, inherited 40 percent of the Mercedes-Benz fortune on condition that he never be seen in any car other than a Mercedes.

Chapter 43

What Did He Leave?

"What did he leave?" was the oft-repeated refrain of an old Irish balladeer's song about an Irish wake. It is also just about the first question everyone asks when they hear someone has died. The curiosity to know how much a person managed to accumulate during his lifetime on this mortal coil may be morbid, but it is universal. The amount involved seems to be of as much interest as is the disposition of the estate. This slight cross section will give an inkling as to how much could be accumulated by various categories of persons. For instance:

The estate of Ailsa Mellon, one of the world's wealthiest women, amounted to $570,648,725. Only about $7,000,000 went for taxes, as the bulk of the estate, $556,634,826, was bequeathed to the Mellon Foundation.

The estate of Joseph Pulitzer, editor and publisher of the St. Louis *Post-Dispatch*, amounted to $2,908,754. On this, federal taxes of $387,569 and Missouri inheritance taxes of $53,928 were paid. Administration expenses were $8,804, attorneys' fees were $62,000, and executors' fees were $86,888. The estate had $266,287 available in cash.

Erle Stanley Gardner, author of the Perry Mason series of detective stories, left a gross estate of $1,795,092.

The estate of Irene Castle, famous ballroom dancer, amounted to $221,202.

Walter Hagen, golf champion, left an estate of $210,238.

George "Gabby" Hayes, Western movie actor, left $111,327.

Herbert W. Hoover, founder and president of the Hoover Vacuum Cleaning Company, left $2,162,479.

Joseph K. Lilly, Jr., grandson of Eli Lilly and Company's founder and chairman of the board, left $57,802,803.

Henry J. Kaiser, industrialist, left $5,597,722.

General Jonathan Wainwright's estate amounted to $72,424.

John Jacob Astor's estate was valued at $150,000,000, making him the richest man in America at the time of his death.

Albert Einstein's estate was valued at $65,000.

Automobile magnate Henry Ford left an estimated $600,-000,000.

At the time of his death, President Kennedy held an estimated $10,000,000 in trusts.

The schedule of property left by General Robert E. Lee indicated that he was worth $38,750.

The residuary estate of John D. Rockefeller was estimated to be $25,000,000.

Theodore Roosevelt's estate was estimated to be $500,000.

George Washington's estate was valued at $600,000.

Charles W. Englehard, multimillionaire industrialist and racehorse owner, left an estate of $250,000,000.

Movie actor Dan Duryea left $288,918.

Jack Carson, comedian, left $189,854.

The estate of columnist Walter Winchell was estimated at between $500,000 to $750,000.

Richard Prentice Ettinger, cofounder of Prentice-Hall publishing house, left an estate valued at $24,000,000.

The estate of John C. Wilson, chairman of Xerox Corporation, was valued at between $10,000,000 and $15,000,000.

Igor Stravinsky, composer, left an estate of $1,250,000, exclusive of archives valued at $3,500,000.

Sherman Mills Fairchild, founder of Fairchild Camera & Instrument Corporation, left an estate in excess of $200,000,000.

Senator Richard B. Russell of Georgia left $1,000,000.

Senator Everett McKinley Dirksen's estate amounted to $302,235.

President Eisenhower left $2,870,005.

Vincent Sardi, founder of Sardi's Restaurant, left an estate estimated at between $100,000 and $250,000.

Robert Watson Goelet, a socialite oil and real estate magnate who died in 1941, left an estate valued at $19,579,316.

Estate executors listed the following deductions: federal taxes, $11,572,348; New York state tax, $2,693,096; Rhode Island state tax, $1,269,859; Utah state tax, $2,717; province of Quebec tax, $6,833; province of New Brunswick tax, $7,898; administrative expenses, $966,000; appraisers' fees, $250,000. After other minor expenses, the amount remaining to the four heirs was $2,808,615. He willed the Ritz-Carlton Hotel at 46th Street and Madison Avenue in New York to Harvard University, free of mortgage and restrictions.